The Well-Referred Dentist

The
Well-Referred
Dentist

The Essential Hidden
Steps to a PROFITABLE &
ANXIETY-FREE PRACTICE

BITA SALEH D.D.S.

NEW YORK

LONDON • NASHVILLE • MELBOURNE • VANCOUVER

The Well-Referred Dentist

The Essential Hidden Steps to a Profitable & Anxiety-Free Practice

Published in New York, New York, by Morgan James Publishing in partnership with Difference Press. Morgan James is a trademark of Morgan James, LLC. www.MorganJamesPublishing.com

ISBN 9781642795615 paperback
ISBN 9781642795622 eBook
ISBN 9781642795639 audio
Library of Congress Control Number: 2019903902

Interior Design by:
Chris Treccani
www.3dogcreative.net

Morgan James is a proud partner of Habitat for Humanity Peninsula and Greater Williamsburg. Partners in building since 2006.

Get involved today! Visit
MorganJamesPublishing.com/giving-back

This book is dedicated to my dental colleagues for their lifelong quest of making a difference in the lives of their patients.

TABLE OF CONTENTS

INTRODUCTION

Why have we been silent for so long?

As dental students we were taught how to not traumatize our patients. This issue was raised in only one or two classes in the entire dental school curriculum, the classes dedicated to delivering painless injections. It was great material and we learned how to effectively deliver painless injections but unfortunately that was all it was.

No one talked about what to do with the patient who has already been traumatized before they walked into our practice(s). We jumped from painless injections to sedation. It's either this or that with no steps in between. In the entire list of dental procedure codes, which is comprised of over 100 dental codes there is only one code dedicated to behavior management – a very broad category usually not covered by insurance plans. Does this mean it is an option to not suffer and if you so choose you have to pay for the expense of the only option presented to you (that being sedation) entirely out of pocket? To do that is expensive and invasive requiring lengthy preparation and recovery.

Mental health professionals have done a great job of researching and writing volumes of books dedicated to fear, anxiety, trauma, and phobia. As dental students we were not recommended any because we needed to learn about dentistry and how to do it extremely well. The question is, "How can the most accomplished dentist in the world treat a fourteen-year-old patient who comes in at the end of the day with an abscess, crying hysterically not because of the excruciating pain they're experiencing, but because they're afraid of the dentist?" Is it really an option for a dentist to tell the parents of this child that they have to take her to a psychologist first to address her fears about dental treatment before they can get her out of pain? On the other hand, if your patient won't open their mouth wide enough, how can you deliver the phenomenal dentistry you have been trained to deliver?

To be fair our training cannot be blamed, because even four years of dental school isn't enough time to teach students everything there is about dentistry. As one semester blends into another, dental students count themselves lucky if they can get a few hours of sleep every once in a while. However, in those sleep-deprived four years, most graduating students are grateful and proud of what they have learned.

Most will go on to hone their clinical skills even further by taking continuing education classes, none of which will address fear and anxiety. They will enter the world as healthcare professionals who are eager to serve. However, what they will face is anger, frustration, or sarcasm, and more from their patients because they don't know that the real cause of their patients' unpleasant behavior is fear and anxiety. These issues show their ugly faces in a myriad of different forms ranging from money and insurance issues to the amount of time it takes to travel to see their dentist.

This is usually where frustration and resentment set in, as the inexperienced dentist will miss the signs of fear and anxiety. They will wonder why some patients do not return or why they no-show for their confirmed appointments. They will often blame themselves and question what they have missed or how they could have done better.

On those occasions when the fearful patient makes it into the dental chair, the missed signs result in a sixty-minute procedure turning into a 120-minute procedure because the patient will not remain still or insists on using the restroom every twenty minutes. The stress of not being able to do their best work and running late for the next patient eats away at the dentist even after their day has ended. In situations such as this it's not uncommon for the dentist to describe their frustrations as mirroring feelings of having their feet stuck in the mud or quick sand. "The harder I tried the further I sank" is a common feeling described by many during times of frustration. These adverse feelings can linger and haunt dental professionals in their sleep showing up as nightmares or a general feeling of having failed, despite their best efforts.

I personally often wondered what my colleagues were doing to handle these unfortunate situations and so I called and went to see a few. The first person I asked was one of my dental school professors who practiced locally. I took him to lunch and asked him for his secret sauce, as it was well known that most of his patients loved him. His answer was "just because patients talk to you, it doesn't mean you have to listen. Just nod your head or say the occasional yes; but mainly ignore them; in one ear and out the other." Another colleague said, "I build a wall around me so thick that nothing they say or do can penetrate." As you're reading this, you might think that these comments seem crass and flippant. Since I knew these two dentists, I knew that they cared deeply about their patients, but this was what worked for them so that they wouldn't have to deal with patient behaviors that were generated from fear and anxiety because after all there was no manual available for that.

What other dentists shared with me was about being tortured by the behaviors of their patients. They felt helpless and frustrated. They went home exhausted and drained only to turn around and do it all over again the next day. Some choose to not look at their schedules because seeing the name of that one difficult patient on their schedule ruins their entire day.

As is evident, both sides are stressed and miserable. The dentist is stressed because he/she can't or doesn't know what to do about these patients and the patient is stressed because each time they walk in a dental office they are triggered and they are afraid. This results in a vicious cycle where the patient won't want to go see the dentist regularly resulting in further deterioration of their dentition, appointments that are more frequent and lengthier and more costly treatment.

Who else is better equipped to treat the fearful patient than their dentist who lives in the trenches of darkness and despair with them?

For some it's easier to block the fear and anxiety of a patient so it cannot be heard or felt. To believe that "this part of you is not my problem" might seem more time efficient to some dentists.

I have often asked myself whether, as dentists, we are healers or just mechanics with a DDS or DMD degree and a great amount of knowledge. To treat human beings with the intent to heal requires courage thereby we are indeed healers and not mechanics. Courage is the ability to do something that frightens one. The letter "c" in the word "courage" relates to curing. The other letters in the word relate to owning, upgrading, restoring, alleviating, grace, and lastly, emending. All these words point to the central theme of healing. I am not defining healing as only curing either. Curing, I would describe as a procedure, which may or may not be done under anesthesia, with a certain limited recovery time. It's what we do in dentistry when we treat the teeth or the gums. It is linear with a predicted outcome.

True healing from the core of a being is multi-dimensional, takes time, and is often painful, in the sense that the pain cannot be dulled by anesthesia. It requires awareness and action not only from the will, but also from every part, every cell, everything that constitutes who we are. Above all else, it requires courage from the patient as well as the healer. The healer has to believe that what seems impossible is actually possible.

To be an exceptional healer is not only about getting a degree from the best program or learning a clever technique or having the best equipment that technology can offer. It's remarkable how much money is spent every year in dentistry for the development of the fastest and the best equipment and yet there is a stark absence of any training for dentists to address dental fear and anxiety.

However, we all know that when a patient is unable to even sit in the chair because of fear, the value of all those technological advancements is equivalent to zero.

You might want to believe that getting through and completing dental school and passing the dental boards is being courageous. I would argue that these achievements are mostly the result of determination and hard work. As you enter the real world, you're asked to be a healer and that has little to do with technology or equipment.

Being an exceptional healer requires the kind of courage that is the hardest to find. It calls for your heart to step in to let your patients know that they are your priority, that you see them and love them in whatever form they have shown up that day, and that all parts of them are safe with you. This has to come from your heart, from the most genuine part of you, so that it can be reflected by every part of your presence.

It requires courage to want and believe that you are the first responder in the face of fear and anxiety. Serving your patients requires a spoonful of courage every second of every day and it continues after hours affecting every decision that you make.

Courage is being willing to see and hear the subtle ways that fear whispers before it takes over and paralyses your patient. Why not face the resistance at the core and cut its legs out before it has time to destroy any chance of a successful doctor-patient relationship?

This book will show you how to create the kind of bond with your patients that is unbreakable, so that they no longer ask whether what you're recommending is covered by insurance or not, or whether they should shop around to find a cheaper office, and there are a thousand other questions asked by patients that are a result of fear. Instead the only thought that crosses their mind is how fortunate they are to have found you because they feel safe with you.

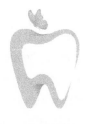

CHAPTER 1:

My Story

I want to congratulate you for being here. For me, writing this book was about peeking around the corner every day and sending you a gift filled with so much gratitude. I want you to know that your patients will feel the depth of this gratitude as well. For the first time in their lives they will view you as their lighthouse instead of a house of horror that causes them fear.

Pursuing this profession for me was not by accident or something that I fell into when looking the other way. Ever since childhood I wanted to be a dentist.

Dentistry to me is a unique combination of art, science, and indescribable beauty. The following describes my love and testament for teeth in a way that only a dentist may understand. As I try to explain the story of teeth in the way that I have witnessed, I find that words fail me in my attempt to capture their uniqueness. The flawlessly efficient way that they function every moment of every day is only recognized and respected by those who understand their way. A significant part of their story includes the truth that they undergo insurmountable stress every day as their humans clench and grind in each and every way. They help us eat and speak and feel confidence in the world and yet we forget to care for them because that requires too much work. Despite the lack of care, they continue to faithfully serve without entertaining the thought of abandoning their post. They patiently tolerate being worn down by the bruxer, who endlessly abuses them throughout the night like no other. Oral health becomes fragile when overwhelmed with this negativity, yet its strength up to this point is nothing short of limitless courage and humility. Teeth are endlessly devoted as they continue to serve us until they can no longer stand the stress of being neglected. It's a world within a world, dependent for its survival, upon loyalty and team-work within its intricate parts. Teeth support and rely on one another for the dance of occlusion to play out perfectly, similar to what musicians in a concert would do to create music together beautifully. They love to dance in balance where very little strength is involved, and yet when viewed as a whole, they're a testament to their dedication to what true strength is all about. Even though each tooth seems fragile on its own, together their strength cannot be denied as a whole. Their beauty is subtle, not loud or crass and yet the beauty of a smile is entirely dependent on all the teeth in the pack. As dedicated as loyal servants, carrying the secrets passed down through generations, teeth are not afraid to use their power to set boundaries when misused or abandoned. As witnessed by anyone experiencing a toothache, the intensity of the pain created by a fractured or diseased tooth is nothing less than the devastation created by a gunshot through the head. Above all teeth are understood and loved only by a privileged few, who spend a lifetime observing, studying, caring, and adoring the details of their smallest curvatures, intricacies, and sensitivities so that they can speak their language, which is pureness and truth.

I have often wondered how could the dentistry that I love doing so much bring those who I have vowed to serve so much fear and trauma. Through the years I realized that there was a reason that I felt the traumas of every patient. As an empath, I had no choice but to find the courage to be in the trenches, experiencing the fear and anxiety of my patients. In order to save myself so that I could continue doing the dentistry that I loved, I had to figure out a way to save my patients, while they sat in my chair, from the trenches.

I was in my mid-twenties when I graduated from dental school. A one-year general dentistry residency followed and that's where my most critical learning took place. It was here that I learned surgery and sedation and most importantly how to do it fast without loss of quality.

Some things in life stay with you forever. One such example happened one day when I walked into the oral surgery clinic where I was assigned and saw the waiting room filled with patients who needed their teeth extracted. There were three of us in the clinic that day. If no other patients were added to the schedule throughout the day, I estimated that we each had to do roughly three extractions every fifteen minutes, which meant fifteen minutes per patient.

My first patient was a lady in her mid-fifties who needed three surgical extractions. She had the deer-in-headlights look, which meant she was so nervous that she couldn't find the words to express her fear or her needs. I slowed down to take the time needed to calm her down before applying a numbing agent. As I was comforting her, my supervising oral surgery resident stopped by at the doorway of my operatory and said: "You need to grow some hair on your chest." I was surprised but not offended by his comment. I knew my patient was too frozen with fear to care so I just chalked it up to that being what was required of me there and so I started to numb the patient. The next time he stopped by, it was fifteen minutes later, at which point I had numbed the patient and managed to get all three teeth extracted with the help of my speedy high-speed drill. It was obvious that I got the job done as was evident by the tooth powder in the operatory; blood splattered everywhere, and pieces of bone and sectioned teeth scattered all over the tray directly in front of the patient.

He said, "Wow, you grew hair on your chest fast!" Soon after he departed, the patient asked if we were done and just as quickly as I said "yes" she fainted. Oxygen was brought in and the assistants took care of her as I walked into another operatory ready to anesthetize the next patient.

It broke my heart to have not had permission to be there for her, either before or after, the treatment. That day I learned that my heart and my ability to show compassion or to be present for a patient who clearly needed to be comforted, were not part of that day or any other day, at least while I was there.

It wasn't until my one-month rotation in the jail ward that I – for the first and only time in my career - felt lacking compassion was useful. The patients awarded me the nickname "Dracula" because by then, I was well trained in hiding my compassionate side. I had to repeatedly stick patients with needles in an attempt to find a working vein to draw blood from.

The choices for a patient needing to undergo dental treatment were either local anesthesia or sedation. If a patient was not able to be cooperative, their dental treatment was scheduled in the operating room under sedation.

Private practice was not the same. The job I procured as an associate dentist in an established medium-size private practice a year later allowed me a few more minutes to develop a relationship with and gain the trust of the patients – however this had to be done quickly and efficiently. At the end of the day, my boss was concerned about two things: production/collection and profits. I did manage to change my boss's viewpoint of me from being described as "she is very presentable" at the beginning of our working relationship to "she's the best associate dentist I have ever had the pleasure of working with" toward the end of our working together.

I never took time off for holidays, never took shortcuts and always made sure that I treated each patient with respect while I delivered impeccable dentistry. I loved dentistry, I loved to learn, and I loved to serve, so much so, that I didn't realize he was paying his hygienist more than he was paying me. I realized I knew nothing about the business of dentistry so I counted myself lucky to have been offered a position right after the completion of my training (even though I had to move to a city where I knew no one) and so I tolerated the low salary for one year until it became clear that our ethical values were so vastly different that there was no choice but to part ways.

This decision was not made easily. It was hard leaving a job that paid for my livelihood despite the unfair salary. However, I knew in my heart that being profitable should not mean compromising patient care.

The only way I knew how to create this type of culture was to own and operate my own practice. While I was looking for a small practice to purchase, I supported myself working for other dentists part-time and covering for emergency care at the local dental society.

Finally, after six months of searching, I found a small practice where the owner was retiring. The purchase went quickly and suddenly I found myself being handed the keys to a small dental practice where the furniture, the paint and the equipment had not been renewed for at least thirty years. But that was all I could afford, and I wasn't complaining.

I remember the moment that the previous owner handed the keys to me and left. I looked around and took in the old musky scent of the place, walked into my tiny private office and burst into tears. I allowed myself the feeling of being overwhelmed for only a few intense minutes. I quickly remembered the old saying: "you need to grow hair on your chest." So, I pulled up my big doctor pants and walked out of my tiny private office into what was now my dental practice. It was a good thing that I didn't allow myself more time to wallow because soon after my first patient stormed in, in a state of panic, with her recently cemented crown in her hands. After evaluating the tooth, it became apparent that there was no sound tooth structure existing above the gum line. This crown should have never been made with these existing conditions. Discovering this truth for myself was a hard pill to swallow but telling this to the patient who had recently paid for a crown, were two vastly different terrains in a mountain of "supervised neglect" that I had to learn to claw my way through.

There were many other patients who came in with similar situations who I had to deliver similar bad news to. Instead of placing blame where it was needed (that being the previous dentist), they walked out thinking I was the one milking them dry of all their money. This is the amazing part that I want you to pay very close attention to. This is where the first face of fear emerges. It is called "fear of change."

As I did my best to describe to them why their recently completed dental work was failing, they chose to believe the retired dentist even though he was long gone. What he had accomplished, which was something I had not yet done, was establishing a trusting relationship with the patients.

For me, the first step toward accomplishing the development of a trusting relationship with these patients, involved realizing the power that "fear of change" had on people. They would rather continue believing that the guy who was their dentist for thirty years had their best interest in mind even though the evidence to the contrary was staring them right in the face. This was my introduction to witnessing "cognitive dissonance."

The truth was that I was a highly accomplished dentist who knew dentistry and knew how to work fast. I was likeable with social skills that granted me the opportunity to be blessed with a large circle of friends. However, my patients saw me as a young pretty little thing who had just gotten out of dental school with a lot of debt. I often wanted to scream, "that's not why your mouth is falling apart." The reality of what I didn't know yet, was how to recognize the signs of fear and anxiety and how to deal with it.

My pitfall was not lacking the knowledge to be an extremely competent dentist, but instead was lacking the knowledge to recognize the signs and how to effectively interact with patients suffering from dental fear and anxiety. If you asked me anything about dentistry, I was able to confidently give you the correct answer. I was able to create the most comprehensive treatment plans meant to bring the patient's dentition to complete health. Unfortunately, these comprehensive treatment recommendations were often not accepted by patients and so remained as being comprehensive only on paper filed in the proper section of the patient's chart. I learned that each time a patient asked, "how much will my insurance cover," it really meant "I'm not accepting all your treatment recommendations and so I'm staying within the confines of my insurance coverage and limitations." Therefore, my comprehensive treatment plan, instead of serving as a roadmap to healthy dentition for the patient, was slayed and sentenced to a future of existing as nothing but artwork on paper filed somewhere in the patient's chart. I was really starting to wonder whether my training had taught me "fantasy dentistry" instead of "real-life dentistry." In "fantasy dentistry" we were taught to do amazing comprehensive dentistry but in "real-life" we had to teach ourselves how to manage the obstacles of patient behavior before we could ever dream of doing the beautiful dentistry that we were taught.

A few years later I was volunteering at the California Dental Association meeting when I was invited to the "wise elders table" where that day's speakers sat. Eagerly I accepted and prepared myself to catch the lifeboat that I was sure the sage advice of these elders would provide me. However, their advice consisted of learning more about dentistry and dentistry alone. I began to realize that helping patients with their fears and anxieties was something no one practiced or talked about. I wasn't even sure myself at the time, of the great effect that patients' fears and anxieties had on a dental practice, but what I did know was that I was tired of my patients not following my recommendations.

Not only did my patients remain unhealthy, but also the production and collection numbers in my business stagnated and did not improve. I went home every day exhausted after working ten-hour days while I took every word and every gesture to heart. I felt everything that my patients felt but I didn't know how to help them. I wasn't able to build a wall so thick that nothing could penetrate. It was as though I was born to feel everything. My personal life was minimal because I was always working, and these were the thoughts that kept me awake at night:

Why can't I connect with my patients?

Why don't they trust me?

Why don't they accept my treatment plans?

Why don't they see that I have their best interest at heart more than anyone else does?

What good is all my expertise in dentistry when I'm not given permission to do what I know best?

I love teeth but I'm not sure how to help the people those teeth belong to. What would it take to win these patients over?

I feel like I'm failing every day. I feel the fear and anxieties of these patients, but they don't talk about it and I don't know how to help them, even if they did talk about it. Because of this my overhead is through the roof and my business is not growing. These problems haunt me day and night. I'm afraid if I don't figure this out, I'll end up losing my practice. Why didn't they teach us about this in dental school? Maybe I should have gotten a psychology degree before applying to dental school.

The answers to the problem of fear and anxiety were nowhere to be found. There was no training and no manual for this huge part of real-life dentistry. So not knowing what to do with the existing patients, I made up for it by spending a lot of money in advertising to bring in new patients. The new patients called and made appointments and came in, but again and again, the same fear and anxiety that I had no idea how to deal with showed its ugly head in the new patients – in a hundred additional different ways.

The truth was that I had to repeatedly remind myself that I was a great dentist. I had small hands and I was gentle and kind by nature, but what good was all that when my patients were too afraid to accept my treatment recommendations. As the thoughts mentioned above ran around in my head, every day I was frustrated that I didn't have the answers to change anything. How do you change a patient's inability to trust their doctor? Although I felt that the fears and anxieties of my patients comprised eighty percent of my practice, I did not have the knowledge base or the expertise to help them so that they could obtain dental treatment with ease and comfort. Regardless of how hard I worked, I often felt as though I had failed. There were many years at the beginning of my career where I had to walk on the edge. I wasn't able to make enough money to pay my loans and overhead and was afraid that I won't be able to stay in business. This was in a time when banks were not lending money to doctors in general, so life was tight. Because I was always working, I didn't have time to socialize or have a personal life. I was frustrated that I couldn't do the dentistry that I was trained to do. Something I had worked so hard for most of my adult life was now making me unfulfilled and unhappy. I felt that if I knew how to help patients with their fears and anxieties then they would accept all my treatment recommendations, they would not cancel or no-show for their appointments and they would not be so dependent on their insurance limitations and coverage. As a result, I would be able to make enough money to pay my bills, grow my practice, and have enough time to have a personal life. I didn't want to instead be married to a practice that consumed every second of my life leaving me exhausted, drained, and unfulfilled.

With the passing of each year I became busier and, and as a result, my earnings increased. And as I gained new patients, their fear and anxiety followed. Each evening when I went home, I was drained and exhausted with no hope that this problem could or would ever change. I figured that this is how it's supposed to be. This is what owning a dental practice and being responsible for patients looks like. This is how it's always going to be. With this realization came much despair because the future did not look satisfying as long as the problem of fear and anxiety remained unsolved.

I have traveled down the road that you might be traveling right now. It might be slightly different but it's nevertheless the same. After travelling down this road for many years I realized I had to go back to school to learn what I had never learned in dental school. I had to learn how to help my patients resolve their fears and anxieties. I knew that for someone like me who wasn't able to build a wall of protection to block out my patient's negative feelings, travelling on this road would be much harder. As I shared my frustrations with others it became more and more clear that these feelings were shared by many other dentists.

This was not an easy decision to make because committing to a decision like this meant that while I continued to practice and run my office, I had to sacrifice all my free time to study and maintain a tight budget to make up for the added expense of tuition. I had reached a fork in the road where I wasn't able to tolerate one more bad day or one more incident where I had no solutions for the fear and anxiety that my patients suffered from. Whether this fear and anxiety appeared as resistance due to lack of finances or lack of time for treatment or inability to communicate properly, it all boiled down to me bearing the responsibility of not being able to help them get healthier in the way that I knew was possible for them.

Fear and anxiety are the root causes of most forms of resistance hindering your relationships with your patients and the success of your business. It's important to understand why this help has to come from you and not an outside person and why it has to be accomplished in a time-efficient manner. There are many variations to the method that I will describe in this book, but keep in mind that the method described here is geared specifically for you as dental health professionals dealing with dental fears and anxieties and is proven to be successful. I'm thrilled that you're here as this training is decades past due.

CHAPTER 2:

Roadmap to Clearing the Triad of Obstacles:

Fears, Anxieties, and Limiting Beliefs

As dentists, every day we must face our patient's fears and anxieties. These fears and anxieties result in negative feelings which show up in different ways in each patient ranging from anger about fees charged to lack of understanding and missed appointments. The cumulative impact of these negative feelings is palpable and damaging for the dentist, the team members, and the practice. It's these reasons and many more why it's wise for dentists to expand the scope of their duties to include anti-anxiety measures so as to not only help their patients, but also improve their own lives, their job satisfaction and their business's success.

In this chapter, you are introduced to energy psychology methods, which can be done in the dental office by the dentist or team member certified and trained in these methods. Included in these methods is the creation of a meridian sequence of tapping, which is significant in finding the original cause of the patient's fear as well as alleviating the charge caused by the fear. Through seven main steps you can help transform the resistance that is caused by fear and anxiety into full compliance and health.

The question of whether these methods are within the scope of practice of dentistry may or may not cross your mind at some point in this book. It's important to address this right away and put your mind to rest so that it doesn't occupy your thoughts and present as an obstacle throughout the book. Many of you have implemented anti-anxiety measures such as relaxation or breathing techniques, offering soothing music, a warm blanket, or holding a patient's hand when the stress gets too much for them. None of this is considered outside the scope of the practice of dentistry. Take it a step further and consider for a moment the potential answers to the questions below: Is helping a patient who has vomited all over the chair, while being sedated with nitrous oxide, within the scope of your practice? Is helping a patient who is having a panic attack while in your dental chair within the scope of your practice? How about helping a patient who is about to faint or has fainted due to severe anxiety? Or the patient who is having heart palpitations or a heart attack due to being overly stressed from fear and anxiety?

I know you're aware of hundreds of adverse or life-threatening situations that can occur when you are the only one who can help a patient suffering in one way or another during the very moment that they are under your care. If they're having a physical reaction, you have been trained in emergency medicine to help them. But what if they're at the stage before having a physical reaction? Isn't helping them considered as being what is required of us as humans in the healthcare field, so that they don't have a physical or emotional or any type of reaction other than pure ease and comfort?

I would recommend letting all your patients know that you're there for them should they need you to help them with fear and anxiety induced by a clinical setting. Let them know that you recommend taking action before a treatment appointment is scheduled to prevent the occurrence of negative feelings. If they are existing patients, you and your team might already know what makes undergoing dentistry hard for them. If they are new patients address this with them as soon as possible. Asking them to complete an anxiety questionnaire is acceptable, but not necessary because you might not get their true feelings as the subconscious mind cleverly masks their fears until there is a real trigger present. Instead of a questionnaire simply seat them in an operatory in a dental chair and ask them this question: "If I told you that I have time in my schedule to start all your treatment right now, what are the first thoughts that go through your mind?" Allow them ten seconds to verbalize their thoughts out loud and write them down in their words. You have just discovered their biggest fears. Take them back into the consult room and now you can have a more real conversation with them about your recommendations before dental treatment is discussed. Ideally you want to discuss your treatment plan after you have helped them resolve their fears, anxieties, and negative beliefs.

If their insurance plan is ending tomorrow or for whatever reason they need their treatment completed right away, you can always use the short protocol discussed in Chapter 14 to alleviate their fears and anxieties. However, we will assume they do not have any pressing desires or circumstances that force them to complete certain or all their treatment as soon as possible.

Just so you don't have to cross any boundaries, do this work with your patients in a consultation room or any private area other than your dental operatories where you perform dental treatment. After discussing with them the benefits of and treatment for alleviating dental fears and anxieties, ask patients to sign an informed consent that you have prepared especially for energy psychology methods.

I refer to obstacles that patients experience as a triad. Imagine a closed triangle with one corner being fear, one being anxiety, and one being limited beliefs. All three corners are interconnected and affected by one another. If one corner of the triangle improves, the other two corners will concurrently improve. Conversely, if one corner is impacted negatively, the other two corners will be further exacerbated as well.

In *Living Your Soul's Purpose*, Hammond and Crowley wrote:

> Trauma has neurological as well as energetic roots. This neurological/energetic symbiosis holds physical pain and illness, disturbed emotion, and irrational limiting thoughts. Trauma, as we understand it in psychology and science today is the interaction of neurology and behavior as a result of being victimized or witnessing a traumatic event. When a current event reminds the person consciously or unconsciously of the original traumatic event(s) the brain gets stuck, so to speak, in

the fight or flight response, and reacts to the emerging fear with anger or isolation. [1]

The fight or flight response as a result of the stimulation of the autonomic response is strongly prevalent in patients with dental trauma, as they are either ready to fight (be accusatory, verbally abusive, combative, and angry toward the dentist or auxiliary staff) and/or are ready to flee (run away). This also comes into play in patients who have never experienced dental trauma, but instead have experienced other traumas such as sexual abuse.

Application of the methods proposed in this book does not erase the memory of the traumatic event, but instead erases the emotional signal attached to the memory by eliminating the disturbance of energy flow in the energetic field.

As knowledge is gained through the years, change in viewpoints has become inevitable. The following rendition of history recounts the different viewpoints that Western Science has adopted of the human body specifically in consideration of the relationship between the mind and the rest of the body. To know history is as important as the discoveries because history teaches us about the importance of walking through life with an open mind and an observant heart. The latter is as important as the knowledge itself because without an open mind and the willingness to observe fully, the discoveries will be missed and will never come to see the light of the day.

---

1   Hammond, Mary, and Crowley, Ruth, *Living Your Soul's Purpose: Wellness and Passion with Energy Psychology and Energy Medicine.* Salem: Global Healing Press, 2008, 35.

Centuries ago science, in an effort to separate itself from religion, adopted the mechanistic reductionist viewpoint, which as explained by Gerber,[2] is based upon viewing the human body as a complex machine where treatment involves surgery and drugs.

Prior to this, Democritus who coined the word "atom" held a similar viewpoint about the nature of life. He described everything, including all organisms, as consisting of various parts. To this day molecular reductionism holds this as the dominant biomedical worldview. However, according to Gerber, the Einsteinian viewpoint, which is based on the discoveries of Albert Einstein, views the human being as a, "multidimensional organism made up of physical/cellular systems in dynamic interplay with complex regulatory energetic fields."[3] The Einsteinian model described physical matter in a solid state to be an illusion of the senses. It defined matter to be a substance composed of particles in which the particles themselves are points of frozen light. The wave/particle duality of matter allows us to consider the human physical structure as having qualities not considered in the mechanistic reductionistic model. Aristotle similarly held that organisms are integral wholes and life processes are autonomous and self-ruling. This view, supporting the field concept of life, is today held by the holistic view.

Since the ancient past (early 1600s), vitalism held that a life force was involved in living matter. This life force, also called vital force, was considered to be a metaphysical entity

---

2 Gerber, Richard, *Vibrational Medicine: The #1 Handbook of Subtle-Energy Therapies*. Rochester: Bear & Company, 2001.
3 Gerber, *Vibrational Medicine,* 2001, 68.

responsible for the living aspect of life. In Chinese medicine it was called "qi" (chi), in Japanese medicine it was called "ki," and in Ayurveda it was called "prana." According to Rubik,[4] these descriptions of life energy originated by personal observations of spiritual practitioners and were based on the nature of consciousness and its interaction with mental, emotional, and physical systems in a metaphysical sense.

Western science, at that time, considered this force (also called consciousness) to be immeasurable and therefore outside the scope of science. While Western science dealt with the dilemma of mind and matter as being separate and unrelated, the East believed in an integrated bio philosophy where the mind was not considered separate from the body. In fact, Eastern medicine held the belief that where the mind goes, *qi* flows, and that is where the blood flows.

Therefore, in the East it is believed that the mind is the controlling factor directing the flow of the vital energy, and in turn the energy affects the flesh. In the 1850s, discoveries in bioelectricity challenged the idea that this life force was immeasurable. Electrophysiology and biochemistry soon replaced the notion of life force with electricity, thereby eliminating the concept of vitalism from biological science.

Gerber wrote that we are beings with both physical and subtle energetic components. He described our physical system as an open system existing in dynamic equilibrium with higher energy systems. "All of these systems are physically superimposed upon one another in the very same space." These

---

4   Rubik, Beverly, "The Biofield: Bridge Between Mind and Body." *Cosmos and History: The Journal of Natural and Social Philosophy 11*, no. 2 (2015), 83-96.

higher energy systems, also called *subtle-energy systems* or *subtle bodies*, play a vital role in the total functioning of the human beings.[5]

These subtle bodies are similar to the physical body in that they are also composed of matter, but differ in the frequency characteristics of matter. In physics it is proven that energies with different frequencies can coexist in the same space without interacting in a destructive manner. Just as radio and TV waves are able to pass through the same space without interfering, the energetic matrix of the subtle bodies can exist as a holographic energy-field template superimposed upon the structure of the physical body.

The subtle body or subtle matter closest but slightly higher in frequency to the physical body is the *etheric body*, which carries information (within its energetic map) that guides physical body's cellular growth. It specifically carries spatial information for guiding the developing fetus in utero as well as structural information for growth and repair in the advent of damage or disease appearing in the adult organism. As such the physical body is not only energetically connected but also highly dependent on the etheric body for cellular guidance, so much so that any disturbance or distortion in the etheric field can cause disease in the physical body. According to Gerber, "Many illnesses begin first in the etheric body and are then later manifested in the physical body as organ pathology."[6]

A brief recount of the Acupuncture Meridian System is discussed here so as to bring understanding of certain key words and systems mentioned throughout the book.

---

5   Gerber, *Vibrational Medicine*, 2001, 119.
6   Gerber, *Vibrational Medicine*, 2001, 121.

The etheric body interacts (via flow of energetic information) with the physical body through specific channels of energy exchange called the *Acupuncture Meridian System*. Acupuncture points are points on the human body that follow an unseen meridian system that runs deep into the tissues of the body. The ancient Chinese theory suggests that **qi** (an invisible nutritive energy) enters the body through the acupuncture points and runs through these meridians, bringing life-giving nourishment of a subtle energetic nature, to deeper organ structures.

The Chinese have identified twelve pairs of meridians that are connected to specific organ systems. The proper functioning of the organ systems is dependent on unimpeded and balanced flow of qi to these organ systems. Blockage or imbalance of energy flow over time will result in dysfunction of the organ systems. During the 1960s, Professor Kim Bong Han led a team of researchers in Korea doing experimental work with the acupuncture meridians of rabbits and other animal models. His research suggested that the meridian network was independent of the vascular network. Kim's findings were later confirmed to be true in humans by the research done by Pierre de Vernejoul and others who suggested the meridians as being a unique and separate morphological pathway.

In the energy psychology methods described in this book you will learn in *seven* main steps how to create a customized meridian treatment sequence, which allows for rapid, effective, and lasting treatment of dental fear, anxiety, and trauma. This clearing of the triad of obstacles is achieved through identifying which meridian pathways are blocked in the individual and the related negative emotion that caused the disruption of energy flow in that meridian. By tapping on specific *acupoints*, while thinking and stating out loud the negative emotion, the proper flow of energy will be resumed.

The result is that your patient will still remember the negative emotion but the fight/flight response will no longer be triggered by that negative emotion.

The entire treatment can take approximately ninety to 180 minutes, which can either be completed in one appointment or a series of three consecutive sixty-minute appointments. Knowing this will allow you to set the appropriate amount of time needed in your schedule.

After gaining permission from the patient to start the treatment, the seven main steps are as follows:

1. Muscle testing to verify the testability of the patient (Chapter 7)
2. Centering (Chapter 8)
3. Finding and clearing psychological reversals (Chapter 10)
4. Finding and treating blocked meridians (Chapter 11)
5. 9-Gamut treatment and the Eye Roll (Chapter 12)
6. Explaining the story to the patient (Chapter 12)
7. Maintenance protocol (Chapter 12)

Chapter 3 describes the diverse ways that fear and anxiety show up in a dental practice. It's important to realize that what keeps our patients awake at night is exactly what *adversely* affects our abilities to help our patients properly and to keep our business viable. It's even more important to care for ourselves, especially if we are empaths, because we run other people's negative feelings through our own bodies as though we are experiencing those negative feelings ourselves. By continually feeling the feelings of others as though it is our reality, we end up feeling exhausted and drained. In addition, you will learn how to truly "see" your patients so that you can identify the red flags of fear and anxiety. It's very helpful for a dentist to recognize the presence of fear and anxiety (in whatever way it presents itself) prior to scheduling a patient for dental treatment.

In Chapter 4, you will discover how patients describe their fears and anxieties in their own words. The definitions of fear, anxiety, trauma, phobia, and limiting beliefs are described along with and how they impact the dental patient and the successful outcome of their treatment and experience in the dental office. The term "triad of obstacles" as introduced in Chapter 2 will be described in more detail, offering an understanding of what is truly in the way of better health for patients who suffer from dental fear and anxiety.

In Chapter 5, I explain the importance of bringing to light the adverse effects of dental fear, anxiety, and negative beliefs, and how to gain permission from the patient to address these negative feelings. We are always obligated to inform our patients about their options, which includes methods that facilitate overcoming these negative feelings.

Chapter 6 contains the steps that a patient is recommended to follow the day before a session to achieve the best results.

Chapter 7 begins the first step of creating a customized meridian treatment by introducing muscle testing as the most reliable way of checking the truth of a statement by asking the body, instead of the mind.

In Chapter 8, the second step is introduced, mainly involving centering and correcting polarity imbalances for your patients as well as yourself.

Chapter 9 discusses the definition of meridian pathways and the effect of proper energy flow vs. obstructed energy flow in manifesting physical disease.

In Chapter 10, the third step is introduced. This chapter begins by explaining the definition of psychological reversals and how to identify them as well as the importance of clearing them in order to obtain truthful answers when muscle testing the body.

In Chapter 11, the fourth step is introduced. This chapter reviews the method by which you can identify which meridian pathways have disrupted energy flow and how to regain proper energy flow through these pathways.

Chapter 12 introduces the final three steps, including how to determine the best maintenance protocol so that the newly created sequence of tapping becomes permanently integrated. It also explains how to trace the disrupted meridian back to the negative feelings that caused the disruption of energy flow thereby showing the patient the root cause of the disruption.

In Chapter 13, six case studies are discussed showing that even though the root cause of dental fear and anxiety differed between the participants (initially exhibiting moderate to high anxiety), the same method performed on all participants resulted in successful and significant lowering of dental fear and anxiety.

Chapter 14 provides a rapid four-minute protocol of tapping on seven acupressure points along with the results of the published research article that led to the discovery of this protocol showing thirty-five percent dental anxiety reduction. This is particularly useful for patients with dental fear and anxiety who have a dental emergency requiring immediate treatment.

Chapter 15 reviews the ethics and the operation details for dental professionals offering this modality to their dental patients.

Chapter 16 discusses the adverse consequences of viewing this book as an interesting subject only to be looked at again on another day. It's through doing that learning is possible, which is why the word "practice" is used any time dentists perform dentistry on their patients. It's irrelevant whether the dentist is one year or thirty years post-graduation. Performing dentistry is always referred to as practicing dentistry or owning a dental office is referred to as owning a dental practice. In this chapter, you will learn that reading this book is a great first step but to master these energy psychology methods requires becoming certified so that you feel comfortable offering and practicing these methods every day on your patients. This is how dentists can make a difference in the lives of their patients who suffer from dental fear and anxiety.

Dentists love teeth and care for teeth deeply, but without loving the human who has the teeth in their mouth, it would be impossible to truly care for teeth. It's important to discover the person that is being treated as someone whose feelings, beliefs and habits determine the success and the longevity of the dental treatment performed by the dentist. To give you an example, consider a patient with gum disease who comes to your office needing treatment for gum disease as well as a full mouth reconstruction. The dentist completes all the treatment and gives the patient detailed instructions for home care as well as recommendation to return every three months for maintenance. If the patient gives in to their feelings more than their commitment to the dentist's home care instructions he/she may forego flossing and brushing at night for drinking wine and falling asleep on the couch or if instructed to wear their nightguard while sleeping, they may decide not to wear the nightguard because they suffer from low self-esteem and are embarrassed to wear one in front of their partner. So this patient's gum disease will be back within a year, if not sooner, along with a few broken teeth if they are a bruxer. As this example shows, getting to know the patient and what drives their habits before starting the treatment is as important as doing excellent dentistry.

Patients who view dental visits through the lens of fear will not care for their teeth and gums at home, shifting the responsibility of their dental health entirely onto the office visit. This is one aspect of patient behavior that is deeply disturbing, hurtful, and personal to a dentist, especially when the dentist does not recognize the source of this behavior. The dentist performs excellent dentistry, but the treatment fails due to many reasons, none of which has to do with the quality of the dentistry that was delivered and everything to do with the patient not following the dentist's recommendations post treatment. The patient, instead of accepting responsibility, points their finger at their dentist placing all the blame of the failing dentistry onto their dentist. This is yet another great reason to know the patient and what drives their habits before starting their treatment.

Recognizing that a patient suffers from fear and anxiety will open a new vista of information for the dentist. It is because of their fears that patients are unable to understand or retain any instructions or information given to them by their dental office. The sympathetic branch of the autonomic nervous system of a fearful patient sitting in the dental chair is functioning on high alert, much the same way that it would function when faced with real danger, such as being within reach of a hungry tiger or being attacked by an armed burglar. When faced with situations such as these, the entire system of a person is consumed with survival, which does not include listening to their dentist talk about post treatment care.

At the very least by recognizing the signs of fear and anxiety and discussing it with the patient before starting the dental treatment you can inform them, in a way that they are able to understand and retain, what will cause the dentistry to fail. By doing so you are inviting them to be fully engaged in their own treatment. This will include offering them sessions to alleviate their dental fears and anxieties as discussed in this book. I have personally never had a patient refuse to do the work for alleviating their dental fear and anxiety, but if one does refuse and you decide to treat their dentition and it ends up failing, the patient has the knowledge to realize their part and their responsibility in the failing dentistry and will find it difficult to blame their dentist for it.

Ideally, we hope that the energy psychology methods will clear any psychological reversals and limiting beliefs and will allow proper flow of energy throughout the body. This will make it much easier for the patient to choose better habits so that caring for their teeth will be effortless instead of being a struggle.

CHAPTER 3:

Recognizing Fear and Anxiety in Patients Determines the Difference Between a Good vs. a Great Dentist

Most dentists spend the majority of their education learning how to be good, if not great dentists. No one, however, teaches them how to help those patients suffering from dental fear and/or anxiety. It's as though it's taboo to talk about dental fear and anxiety. Maybe if they don't talk about it they don't have to admit that it exists. The reality is that it exists in variable degrees in eighty percent of dental patients (at least those are the ones who seek dental treatment), which is not a small percentage. There is an unknown percentage of patients who never seek treatment due to their fears and anxieties.

Dentists inherently have an intense desire to not only help their patients, but to do so with the utmost perfection. This is woven in the fabric of their being. The treatment that a dentist completes on a patient's dentition shapes his/her reputation throughout the dental community. It is undeniably satisfying to receive compliments from our patients but receiving compliments from our colleagues creates a moment of pride that is savored and not easily forgotten. When we go home at the end of the day, we often don't think about bragging that we made a certain amount of money but if we did outstanding dentistry, we can't wait to show the pictures and share the results with our peers. This is how we were trained. We were trained to have pride in our work because we were trained to do it so well. This is the culture in which we were educated. So, when dentists get frustrated because a patient is uncooperative due to dental fear and anxiety, it's because they're unable to do their best work.

The outcome of treatment is always directly proportional to the cooperation of the patient during and after treatment. When an ideal treatment outcome is compromised due to dental fear and anxiety, dentists often feel that they have failed their patients because they could not help them or were unable to do their best work, regardless of how much money they did or did not make.

In his book Life Energy, the Australian psychiatrist, John Diamond described the patients that he could not help as not having the will to be well.[7] When a patient has experienced a negative emotion such as fear or anxiety or trauma, their life energy diminishes and so does their will to be well. As a result, despite the dentists' best efforts, the patient will not get well.

The desire that most dentists share in caring for their patients is equal to their desire for being entrepreneurs and owning their

---

7   Diamond, John, *Life Energy: Using the Meridians to Unlock the Hidden Power of Your Emotions.* St. Paul: Paragon House, 1985.

own businesses. Their dream does not include permanently working for someone else or building someone else's dream business. One of the reasons that they endure the hard work, the long sleepless hours and the expense of a dental education is to have independence, to be their own boss, and to be the one in charge of their lives. It's because of this deep desire for independence that upon graduation or a few years after, they naively embark on running a business they know nothing about.

Knowing how to operate and manage a successful dental practice is important but what is equally as important is recognizing the many faces of fear and anxiety and how it shows up in your patients. By doing a deepening practice called "teacher of the heart" you will learn how to truly "see" your patients so you can identify the red flags of fear and anxiety. Even if you do this exercise only once, the importance of it will show up in every day of your life.

Find a comfortable chair with your feet on the ground and take a few deep breaths. With each in breath take in the pure loving energy of the earth and with each out breath let go of any distractions or busyness from earlier in the day. Make sure your out breath is twice as long as your in breath. As you continue with your breathing, go back in your memory to a time when someone in your past embodied the characteristics that you recognize a teacher of the heart would have. As you're considering your teachers of the heart reflect upon what made them special to you? What qualities do they embody that you would like to step into as you read the chapters in this book and as you live the days of your life practicing dentistry on humans who want to be seen as the amazing and whole individuals that they truly are, despite how they show up in your office.

The following was my response when I did this exercise:

When I was a fourth-year dental student I was treating a patient with a challenging treatment plan. The clinical professor overseeing my work that day was specialized in the field of prosthodontics and had witnessed my clinical work for two years. I was not feeling well that day, but I was trying to push through. As I was preparing a tooth for a crown, I overestimated the angle of my preparation and accidentally exposed the nerve canal. I explained what had happened to my patient and then informed my clinical professor. I asked both to excuse me for a moment because I needed to go somewhere where I could release the tears that were weighing heavily under my eyelids. With their permission I quickly ran into the rest room and cried for the first time in four years. I knew I had to be done within seconds, so I didn't allow myself time to really feel how disappointed I was. I wiped my eyes and when I returned to the clinical floor, my professor called me over and said: "Dr. Saleh, what happened to you today could have happened to any one of your professors including myself. Don't give this a moment's thought. Know that you're one of the best students here and you have earned everyone's respect. Take a moment if you need to and then start the root canal on your patient."

What made him special to me was that he wasn't swayed by one bad accident. He saw the truth of who I was and reminded me of that truth. He saw me and was witness to how upsetting this incident was for me and acknowledged how hard on myself

I was. He redirected me back to my real self with kindness, confidence, and compassion. He stood up for the real me as I lost myself in that difficult moment. He stood in genuine unconditional acceptance of me when I couldn't.

I often remember this person on my good days, difficult days, and just about every day. These are the qualities that he embodied that I would like to step into:

1. Be willing to be – fully – in loving presence of myself and my patients despite what shows up
2. Be more patient and forgiving of myself so that I can work with my patient's impatience without losing my center
3. Rise above the challenges facing me in the moment and see the bigger picture
4. Be fully in acceptance
5. Stand in my own dignity
6. Embody a presence that is welcoming and kind

As you do this exercise, you'll understand that the qualities that the teachers of your heart embody are the same ones that your patients want from you.

· When your patients are overcome with fear and anxiety, they may show up in ways that do not embody who they really are. They may be impatient, angry, critical, petty, rude, and argumentative, and the list goes on. You can even enforce your own boundaries as long as you hold them in a loving space regardless of which part of them has shown up in that moment.

The bottom line is: "Love your patients regardless of how they show up."

Fear and anxiety can show their presence in multiple ways. Patients will no-show or cancel or be late for their appointments. They will have millions of questions about what is covered by insurance and why they have to pay their copay. They will shop around or won't pay their dental bills. When you are forced to enforce your boundaries such as insisting on holding them accountable for paying their bills, they will retaliate by writing a one-star negative review about you on Yelp and any other online review platforms that they can find. They will talk incessantly before or during the treatment. They will need to use the rest room every fifteen to twenty minutes. They will cry and children will scream. They do not listen and will not retain much when you speak to them (offering guidance and instructions) and this is where misunderstandings will happen. They will not get numb easily and will require more and frequent injections of anesthetic. Then they will complain about how long it took for the anesthetic to wear off after they left the office. They will complain about the length of treatment. They will grab the handles of the dental chair and will constantly fidget. They may move their head away from the dentist in a jerking fashion or will refuse to open their mouth wide enough or will keep their chin down making it more difficult for the dentist to access the teeth. They will complain about neck pain and shoulder pain during and after treatment. They will continually move their feet around. They will be critical of your office and they will go as far as telling you what to put on the walls or the ceiling. However, if you ask them to close their eyes and tell you which color your walls are, they will not remember. When they speak, they face your assistant and not you, in an attempt to distance themselves from you. They will cough and need water frequently. Their mouth will feel dry and yet they will constantly feel the need to swallow. They will become frustrated when they can't swallow because their mouth is numb. They will ask you to squirt water in their mouth just when you need a dry space to make your impression. They will gag or get frustrated with the smell and taste of the materials you're using. They will dictate treatment. They will question your knowledge, expertise, and experience. They will not be able to distinguish between you and the original trauma that caused their fear and anxiety. They will complain about the noise of the drill or the music you're playing and if you're not playing any music, they will tell you that you should. No matter how you try to please them they will find something to complain about. The years of neglect show up in their dentition as missing or broken teeth, the presence of extensive caries and/or gum disease.

If the dentist misses the red flags of fear and anxiety being present and dives head first into recommending treatment, they will never see the patient return to their office. They will always wonder what happened to that patient who needed all that treatment and never returned. They will continually question their own competence and will feel that they somehow failed.

I made this mistake once with a gentleman who was in his early fifties, obese, and required extensive dental treatment. His wife, also a new patient, came in with him so that they could hear each other's treatment recommendations together. When I reviewed his, I also recommended that he makes an appointment to see his physician about his high blood pressure before initiating the proposed treatment recommendations. After hearing all my recommendations, they both walked out while laughing out loud and asked for their records on their way out. I was deeply offended at their disrespectful manner and did not mind getting their radiographs duplicated for their departure. Three months later the wife called my office requesting an appointment for herself only. She said she wanted to get her treatment done and also mentioned that her husband had passed away from a heart attack. Being a young dentist at the time, not knowing about the red flags of fear and anxiety, I chose not to be her dentist. When she asked why, I instructed my assistant to tell her that it had everything to do with her disrespectful behavior during her last visit. Patients often don't remember their behavior during the time that they are overcome with fear and anxiety.

The trickiest face of fear and anxiety shows itself when the patient is unable to distinguish their current dentist from the original traumatic event. An example of this was a patient who was in her mid-fifties and was referred by her husband, who was a long-term patient of the practice. She was an engineer and very well educated. She would refer her family to me but was never happy during or after treatment. In fact, I was always surprised that she kept coming back and kept referring family and friends. It was a complete puzzle to me. One day I prepared two of her teeth for crowns. She called me afterward and complained because she felt that she was "traumatized." I was blown away at her choice of this word because I usually went out of my way to make sure her treatment would go with the utmost ease and comfort. I felt that regardless of all my efforts to keep her happy at each appointment, it was never enough.

When I saw her next, I brought this up to her and suggested that if she truly feels that I traumatize her I will help her find another dentist of her choice. She gawked at me with surprise and said, "If I wasn't happy with you I wouldn't keep coming to you or I wouldn't refer my family and friends." She continued, "Dental treatment is always traumatizing for me."

If I had not discussed this with her, I wouldn't have ever known this truth. She could not distinguish between the original traumatic event and me. Eventually though she found a petty reason to leave my practice and I never saw her again. This example is from my earlier years in practice, and yes, I would have most likely done things very differently with her if I had identified the red flags of fear and anxiety in a timely fashion.

If you fail to recognize these red flags you will lose the patient or you may want to lose the patient. Your treatment recommendations will not be accepted in full. If you spent money advertising (to attract this patient to your office) it would be wasted. You may even get a bad review because misunderstandings are very likely to happen when a patient suffering from fear and anxiety becomes triggered. When you see this patient on your schedule your day will be ruined and after you do see them you may want to quit your job and go home because the aggravation won't seem worth it. You will always wonder what happened or what you could have done to have a better outcome. They will eventually end up going to another dentist and another one and each dentist will wonder why the patient that they bend over backward for won't stay. You will concentrate all your efforts on bringing in new patients and the cycle will repeat itself again and again.

When the dentist misses the red flags of fear and anxiety, one of the most commonly affected areas of misunderstanding for the patient occurs in the area of finances. The patient might feel that the dentist overcharged them or didn't properly inform them about their insurance coverage. They will not understand why they have to pay anything out of pocket because they believe insurance should cover all of their treatment or at least a good portion of it. They will feel that perhaps insurance wasn't handled properly and instead of blaming the low insurance coverage offered by their employer they will blame the dentist instead. They will wonder why this was not discussed with them in detail prior to the start of treatment. They will feel wronged and not cared for. This may be reason enough for them to start looking for another dentist. When they receive multiple calls from the dental office to pay their balance they are so upset and confused by the bills that they might choose to ignore the calls. When finally, they are sent to collection, they will feel justified to write the most damaging one-star negative review on Yelp and every online review platform they can find. In their mind they need to warn everyone about the office that treated them so poorly.

Fear of the unknown is another significant trigger for a patient who suffers from dental fear and anxiety. If pain is added to this equation it is enough to paralyze the individual. The above example is only a fraction of what can go wrong in the doctor-patient relationship. By recognizing the red flags of fear and anxiety and offering to help alleviate these negative feelings, the dentist can make a significant difference in a patient's life by guiding the patient properly from the very start, breaking the ugly chain of fear and anxiety, winning them over, and having them rave about their new dentist instead of creating an unnecessary enemy.

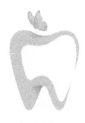

CHAPTER 4:

The Different Ways That Trauma, Negative Beliefs, Fear and Anxiety Affect the Patients in a Dental Practice

I t is important to define the terms fear, anxiety, phobia, and trauma. Draper and James as cited by Öst and Skaret defined fear as being a "normal emotional response to objects or situations perceived as genuinely threatening."[8] Öst and Skaret,[9] further elaborated that this fearful response prepares the individual for a normal preventive reaction of fight or flight by activating the sympathetic branch of the autonomic nervous system. Fear, being considered a rational behavior is slightly different from anxiety.

8   Draper, Thomas W., and James, Rebecca S., "Preschool fears – Longitudinal sequence and cohort changes." *Child Study Journal* 15 (1985), 147-56.
9   Öst, Lars-Göran, and Skaret, Erik, *Cognitive Behavioral Therapy for Dental Phobia and Anxiety*. West Sussex: John Wiley & Sons, Ltd., 2013.

Öst and Skaret wrote that anxiety and fear have similar physical and behavioral components, except that anxiety occurs without a present triggering stimulus. Often the reason for the presence of anxiety is due to the individual anticipating future events by associating them with previous negative experiences. Even though anxiety may be estimated as priming for a future fear response, because it occurs in the absence of an immediate threat, the response is considered irrational. When the anticipatory anxiety reaction is strong and irrational, it may be regarded as phobia, which is a clinical mental disorder. "Among the criteria are: subjects display an extreme and persisting fear of clearly discernible objects or situations, avoidance behavior, and interference with daily life."[10]

These are the steps (not essentially in order) of how anxiety creeps in for a patient. They have a dental appointment the next day and they know rationally how important this appointment is for them. They know it will take ninety minutes as an example and they have agreed to it. They know that when you asked them if they get nervous before the appointment they said "no" because at that time they were not nervous or afraid but today is a different story. As they go about their day their thoughts are racing. Their mind is working so fast that they can't keep up so they're making mistakes. They're forgetting their wallet or forgetting where they put their keys. They will wonder if someone else has taken over the steering wheel of their mind and emotions because it's obvious that they're not in charge. Their mind is starting to go blank and now their heart is racing. They want to call the dentist but don't because they think it's so silly to bother them just for this. They think maybe they're

---

10   Ibid.

falling ill so they try to rest but they can't rest. They will not sleep the night before their dental appointment and they won't eat an adequate meal.

This patient will either cancel their appointment or will no-show or if they do show they will be in such a state of frenzy that you will not be able to do your best work. You will spend most of the allocated appointment time trying to calm them down while they try to talk you into a faster and cheaper alternative that is not your recommended treatment. As a result, you will be stressed for the entire duration of the treatment and the adverse feelings will remain with you all day casting its shadow on the remaining patient appointments of the day.

Most offices call their patients twenty-four to forty-eight hours in advance to remind them of their appointments. If you have already discussed the symptoms of anxiety with your patient, when your office makes the reminder call, you can also remind the patient to call your office if they experience any anxiety prior to their appointment. The discussion before setting any appointments incudes letting your patients know not to dismiss the feelings of anxiety as "silly" or unimportant because they are real and important and you want to be there to help them if it happens. To take this a step further, describe what those symptoms are: a racing mind, racing heart, not being able to relax or sleep, not being able to focus, forgetting things like keys or wallet, feeling of doom and gloom, feeling chaotic, or feeling frozen and not able to make any decisions, all for no actual reason. After learning the methods presented here you will be able to help them very quickly if the need arises. Instead of having a no-show or a last-minute cancellation, or trying to forcefully do some kind of treatment for a very stressed-out patient whose blood pressure and blood glucose levels are all over the place, you will be able to complete your recommended treatment with ease and comfort and the patient will forever be grateful and loyal to you.

I had a patient who was the poster example of an anxious patient when she first came to my office. After I gained her trust, she would fall asleep and snore in my dental chair even when I drilled on multiple teeth. She would tell her husband who always complained about the expense of her dental treatments: "You better pay every cent of her bill because I'm not going to anyone else." So, her husband always paid her bills. As hard as the husband tried, he couldn't put a price on his wife's happiness when she returned home from the dentist's office. In addition, she brought me lemons from her garden and each holiday she sent us gifts and cookies. It's a gift of love that a patient bestows on us when they trust us and each one becomes special to us in their own unique way. However, it's never a finite process and certainly not one to be taken for granted. It's a daily process that is kept alive by a watchful eye, caring heart, and a curious ear.

Gallo explained trauma as being "not only about awful events, but about the attachment in the aftermath of the events. It is attachment at many levels that accounts for trauma." These levels of attachment include traumatic events, perception, neurology, chemistry, information, energy, consciousness, and spirit. Trauma can be eliminated through the application of modalities such as energy psychology whereby the structure of the trauma energy field is substantially altered or collapsed.[11]

---

11 Gallo, Fred. "Energy Psychology and the Resolution of Trauma. 5th International Congress for System Constellations." Accessed May 4, 2005. http://energypsych.com/Home/Readings.

If you Google for the percentage of the American population exhibiting dental fear and anxiety you will find that the highest percentage noted is fifteen percent. Tellez, Kinner, Heimberg, Lim, & Ismail as cited by Saleh, Tiscione, & Freedom stated that dental anxiety affects ten to twenty percent of the U.S. population.[12] Any clinical dentist who has practiced full time for at least one year will tell you that this number is closer to eighty percent rather than twenty percent.

The following is how patients describe their fears and traumas in their own words:

My parents forced me to go to the dentist. Even though I didn't want to, I was told I had to. The dentist strapped me in the chair and forced me to behave. I was not allowed to speak. They did not listen to me when something hurt. I kept feeling pangs of sharp shooting pain, but they told me to just be a good patient and behave. The needle was huge and it hurt upon insertion and as it moved through my tissues. I wasn't completely numb and I could feel pain when they were drilling on my tooth. When they numbed me, I hated feeling numb and out-of-control. The bright overhead light was shining right in my eyes and they were very close to my face, invading my private space as though it was normal to do

---

12 Tellez, Marisol, Kinner, Dina G., Heimberg, Richard G., Lim, Sungwoo, and Ismail, Amid I., "Prevalence and correlates of dental anxiety in patients seeking dental care." *Community Dentistry and Oral Epidemiology* 43, no. 2 (2015): 135–42. doi:10.1111/cdoe.12132. Quoted in Saleh, Bita, Tiscione, Monica, and Freedom, John. "The Effect of Emotional Freedom Techniques on Patients with Dental Anxiety: A Pilot Study," *Energy Psychology Journal*, 9, no. 1 (2017): 26-38. doi 10.9769/EPJ.2017.9.1.BS.

so. I felt awkward when they touched my face and had their fingers in my mouth. The noise of the drill and/or the ultrasonic instrument used to clean the teeth was too loud, piercing, and unexpected. They never explained anything, so I didn't know what to expect and I was afraid of the unknown. I felt out of control especially when I could not swallow and felt as though I was choking and gagging. Because my saliva was sucked out so much my mouth constantly felt dry and this made swallowing unnatural and difficult. There was always bad news, one thing would lead to another and a short appointment would turn into a very long appointment. Nothing good ever happened when I went to the dentist. X-rays hurt and made me gag. It tasted bad and smelled bad. The scraping of the teeth with metal instruments felt like nails on the chalkboard. I hated feeling confined to the chair and being asked to not move. It was hard to keep my mouth open and afterwards my jaw, neck and shoulders always hurt. It was inconvenient in terms of time, cost, and comfort.

Negative thoughts and beliefs can adversely affect a correctly functioning mind-body-energy system. A belief is something that you strongly believe in, so much so that it affects your thoughts about yourself and the world around you. Typically, when someone wants to describe their beliefs, they will start the sentence with "I" or "I am." If the stated belief allows the person to function optimally in the world, to consider their choices while remaining connected to their strength and resilience, it is called a "positive belief." An example of a positive belief is "I am smart and resourceful."

A belief becomes limiting when it adversely affects one's ability to function and achieve long-sought goals. Negative beliefs can either be narrow and affect only certain specific aspects of life (such as "I'm a poor communicator") or wide and affect a large range of areas (such as "I don't deserve to be happy and loved").

A blocking belief is a type of negative belief that adversely affects one's mind-body-energy system. Some blocking beliefs are clear to the individual and some are hidden below the person's awareness. Blocking beliefs take away one's ability to be fully present in the moment while considering one's choices and making healthy decisions.

Most blocking beliefs are learned in the former years of one's life from family experience. An example of the formation of a blocking belief is as follows: an eleven-year-old is helping his mother make hot chocolate on the stove. The phone rings and the mother leaves the kitchen to answer the phone in the adjacent room. The child touches the hot stove and burns his hand so bad that he has to be taken to the emergency room. This is a rendition of what the child has experienced. The negative belief that he will carry is "Stoves are not safe and because stoves are in the kitchen, kitchens are not safe." Therefore, for the rest of his life he feels uncomfortable in a kitchen and the thought of stoves causes him to tremble and break out into a sweat. This negative belief is a blocking belief because it limits his ability to cook for himself and his family. He is unable to enjoy time spent in the kitchen and is unable to buy a house where the kitchen flows into the family room as an open concept. He either eats out all the time or eats unhealthy fast food. As a result, he is overweight and has developed diabetes type II. Another example is a child who was forced to go to a dentist who extracted a primary tooth prematurely without waiting long enough for the tooth to be completely numb. Therefore, the child is traumatized and will form the limiting belief that "dentists and their offices are not safe." The traumatized child's beliefs were justified because the dentist did not provide a safe environment for him. However, as an adult he can choose to go to a different dentist, but he doesn't because he believes all dentists are unsafe. This blocking belief stops him from getting adequate dental care and he ends up losing all his teeth and gets dentures. This results in the patient being embarrassed about his appearance and affects his self-confidence. Since he is in sales, his lack of confidence prevents him from getting promotions and he is continually afraid of being fired.

Patients who are unable to get regular dental care suffer in physical, psychological, and social terms. Physical in the sense that they are in chronic pain and suffer from infections, psychological in the sense that they feel embarrassed and shameful that they cannot get over their fear, and social in terms of not wanting to smile or socialize due to low self-esteem.

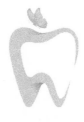

CHAPTER 5:

Gain Permission from the Patient to Treat Before Beginning Treatment

This is the most important chapter in this book. Gaining permission to treat is the most powerful part of your relationship with a patient and, more than anything else, it dictates how successful you will be as a dentist and a business owner.

Dentists practice conventional dentistry extremely well by diagnosing the patient's dentition and recommending treatment. What I have always loved about dentistry is the voluminous amount of evidence-based research that guides us and is abundantly available throughout our career. A diagnosis is made by listening to the patient recount their symptoms followed by examining and analyzing the dentition for proper functioning. This is often achieved with the help of various tools such as x-rays. Once all the information is gathered a proper diagnosis is made and treatment recommendations follow. Treatment often involves restoring the function, integrity, and morphology of the tooth. This is accomplished by debridement of the areas that are diseased, decayed, or fractured, and replacement with either a filling or a crown. Of course, this is a very simplified version of treatment. After a few months or years when the same disease recurs the treatment advances to the next level involving a filling to be replaced by a crown, or a root canal in addition to a crown, and finally an extraction followed by an implant or a fixed bridge. This methodology often depersonalizes the patient even as it treats the disease. Often dentists are not educated to treat the inner life of a person in crisis. Sometimes patients need to know how to live and care for their teeth between office visits or even how to be fully present during the office visit. Marc Barasch found that what patients might need more than anything is for someone to ask: "What help do you need?"[13]

Building trust requires your ability to unfold the truth and state it in a way that your patient understands. Asking a patient whether they are fearful or have anxiety around dental treatment is often not the best way to get a truthful answer. It's not that your patients are purposefully lying to you but often times their fears are so deeply buried in their subconscious mind that they are not fully aware of it.

I had a long-term patient who had severe anxiety around dental treatment. She did fine with exams, x-rays, and cleanings but if the drill was used, she did not do well. It was so bad that I had to prescribe valium for her to take as premedication before her dental visits and have a friend drive her to her appointments and back. Despite going through this each time she needed dental treatment, when asked to make similar preparations

---

13 Barasch, Marc I., *The Healing Path: A Soul Approach to Illness.* New York: Tarcher/Putnam Books, 1993.

(pre-medicate with valium and arrange for a ride) for her next dental treatment, she would look at me as if I was nuts. She was unable to remember how fearful she was until the day before her appointment.

Unfolding the truth and stating it in a way that the patient understands begins at the initial visit when you're doing the exam. Ideally, this would be done if there were no urgent need present to treat right away. Use the technology that is available to you to your advantage. Take lots of intra oral photos, but more importantly, video the exam and the findings as you state them out loud and when done send it to the patient. As an example, instead of saying: "Number three: Buccal caries, occlusal wear and gingivitis", say out loud: "Tooth number three has a lot of decay with moderate amount of wear on top of the tooth making the tooth more prone to fracture, there's also moderate bleeding and the gums look unnaturally red and swollen."

By the time you're done with the appointment your patient has heard the findings and their curiosity is fully piqued to know more. Even if they didn't hear everything because they need more time to process, they can watch the video later with their husband or wife or significant other.

Then you can ask them questions such as: "What do you think the cause of all this wear is? Or did you ever notice your gums bleeding so much?" The patient's answers to these questions reveal their level of awareness, negative beliefs, or any negative past experiences. It prevents them from checking out during the exam process, because you want them to be engaged. Being engaged in the process means they will remember the information presented to them better and allows for improved awareness of the condition of their dentition.

Use as many analogies as possible to describe the condition of their dentition. As an example, if they say, "My gums have always bled. I just thought I was brushing too hard." To help them understand better you can use an analogy such as: "Imagine your gums as being your fingers and your teeth as being your nails. When you clean your nails, your fingers don't bleed and neither should your gums when you clean your teeth." The more you ask questions during this phase the more you lay the foundation for your patient to better understand your treatment recommendations when you present them. At the end of this first visit, ask the patient whether they want to place a Band-Aid on their teeth and gums or they want treatment that makes them healthy and lasts a long time. In your own words explain to them that doing the latter requires mutual cooperation and teamwork where you will both look for any past negative beliefs or feelings that have caused blockages in the flow of energy that is so crucial for the body to stay healthy. To discover this will require a ninety-minute appointment where you will use a combination of energy psychology methods such as Emotional Freedom Techniques and Thought Field Therapy to not only identify but also to resolve any blockages in their energetic system that is contributing to what is causing their gum disease or their teeth breaking as an example."

Let them know that you can get them healthy but remaining healthy requires them to not only show up but to also be actively involved in the treatment before and after the dental work. The methods described herein can be instrumental in preventing the occurrence of disease or work alongside conventional dentistry in supporting the patient's healing.

What is as important if not more so than the patient's diagnosis is the patient's story, which is where the real suffering exists. These methods uncover the story and often that allows the dentist to begin the dental treatment and along with the patient's efforts in home care ensure the longevity of that treatment. As with any healing modality the patient's permission to receive the treatment is paramount in their healing process.

As you can see you will not be discussing their treatment plan until after this appointment. If they inquire about your treatment recommendations, you can show them the photos that you just took as a reminder of what is going on in their dentition but let them know as an example that if you make a crown right now for this tooth that is fractured, they will go on to break this crown again and again if the underlying stress is not resolved first. Make them this appointment within one week. Be sure to give them the patient instructions that I will review in the next chapter so that they know how to prepare for this appointment. In addition, review the informed consent for the next appointment and ask your patient to sign it and provide them with a copy if they so wish to have.

As the patient leaves your office, they have received a video of their appointment (which you will also download into their records) showing you reviewing your findings, they know that you care for their wellbeing beyond only their teeth, and they know that you were willing to listen and truly see them for who they are. They will be comforted by the fact that they have finally found a real holistic dentist. By this point you will have gained a tremendous amount of trust prior to presenting your recommendations for dental treatment.

The protocol I will recommend here is essential for starting their next appointment:

Since you have asked the patient to drink plenty of water before their appointment, it is best to ask them if they need to use the restroom before beginning the session so that they're not distracted by a full bladder during the session. Because energy flows best in a well-hydrated body, get them a large glass of water to drink from during the session. Ask them to remove any jewelry or watches that they might be wearing and place these along with their phone that is turned off in a safe place outside the room. The reason is that these items can interfere with proper energy flow and the successful outcome of their appointment. Ask them if they are comfortable with a light touch on their arms and shoulders. If they are, ask them to sit in a chair with their feet comfortably resting on the floor. Let them know that during the appointment it is best to always look at your shoulder or beyond instead of right into your eyes as you don't want your energy to affect theirs. Verbally ask them permission to start. Once they say "yes," ask them to state their full name out loud three times. Doing so will allow them to give you permission not only physically but energetically as well. To bring them into the present moment ask them to take one full in-breath and follow that with one out-breath that is twice as long as the in-breath. Repeat five times. With every in-breath ask the patient to bring in the pure energy of the earth and with every out-breath let go of any busyness from earlier in the day or whatever it is that they need to do for the rest of the day. Inviting them to be present in the moment is essential.

CHAPTER 6:

Proper Preparation of the Patient in Advance of Their Session

The following is a list of recommendations that patients can follow to properly prepare themselves for the Energy Methods appointment. As a courtesy the team member who makes the appointment reminder call to patients can spend a few additional minutes reviewing these recommendations or the list can be given to patients at a prior appointment.

1. Be sure to get a full eight hours of sleep the night before the appointment.

2. Eat a meal one or two hours before the appointment that includes protein and some carbs. An ideal breakfast would be eggs along with some oatmeal; an ideal snack would be apples and peanut butter; a good lunch would be chicken and a salad with some rice or a potato. You want your patient to have a steady blood sugar and have

enough sustenance to keep them going in flow for the duration of the appointment.

3. Do not drink alcohol or any caffeinated beverages the day of your appointment.

4. Do not wear any jewelry or watches and be prepared to leave your phone on airplane mode for the full duration of the appointment.

5. Wear loose fitting clothing with shoes that can be easily taken off or are comfortable enough to so that you can place your feet on the floor.

6. If you have any reservations about being touched on the shoulders or the arms, please let us know before your appointment.

7. It's important to be hydrated with water so drink one eight-ounce glass of water every sixty minutes the day before and the day of your appointment.

8. Take all your prescribed medications as directed by your physician.

9. Make sure you don't schedule an appointment right after your session. Should the session need to go longer we want you to not feel rushed.

10. It is often best to engage only in light activity or go home to rest after the session.

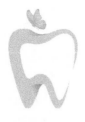

CHAPTER 7:

Muscle Testing Is One of the Most Reliable Ways of Discovering the Truth

In the energy psychology methods described in this book muscle testing is used as the preferred method for testing whether a statement is true for the patient or not. The reason muscle testing is relied upon as the truth indicator is based on the belief that the human body is a much more reliable source of true information than the mind. Muscle testing allows us to bypass the complexities of the mind. Any time an individual makes a false statement, they will experience a physical reaction, which is evident in the strength of their muscles. The muscles of the body weaken in response to a false statement and will strengthen in response to a true statement. This is why when someone wants to deliver bad news, they will always ask the person receiving the news to be seated because they inherently know that it is highly likely that the bad news will weaken the body and the person receiving the bad news may fall.

Applied kinesiology (also called muscle testing) was originally founded in the early 1960s by George Goodheart, an American chiropractor from Detroit, Michigan. His approach addressed physical and mental problems by manually muscle testing and applying holistic concepts. In this groundbreaking healthcare system, he combined methods from chiropractic, physical therapy, and Chinese medicine, and developed a signature method to diagnose and treat a wide variety of illnesses both physical and mental in nature. Applied kinesiology was the first in the Western healthcare sciences to have realized the importance of the mind-body connection in health and well-being. In applied kinesiology, Goodheart tested the strength of different muscle groups and associated certain muscles with specific acupuncture meridians. He discovered that when a muscle tested "weak" it meant that the meridian (energetic pathway in the body) that it was associated with was out of balance. Once the meridian imbalance was corrected, the muscle would test "strong."

Intuition and self-esteem are significant aspects of the holistic model of healthcare. Intuition is a gut feeling that allows us the ability to dial into our surroundings with heightened sensitivity. Some people are naturally intuitive, meaning that they are born with the gift of intuitive or symbolic sight, and those who are not born with it have the ability, just like any other skill, to develop and fine tune it.

Self-esteem plays an important part in the blossoming and the accuracy of intuition. Self-esteem and belief in one's intuition allows one the necessary personal power and confidence to develop one's intuitive ability, as well as, one's intuitive accuracy. It is intuition at work when a dentist has a gut feeling that something is off with the patient in their chair before any physical signs confirm this feeling. If the dentist does not have the necessary self-esteem to trust their intuitive feeling, they may well be calling 911 when a few minutes later their patient presents signs of a heart attack. One example of my intuitive feelings was knowing, a few minutes before my patients did, that their anesthetic was about to wear off. I would stop drilling and I would ask my patients if they were starting to lose their numbness and sure enough the answer was "yes, I think so, how did you know?" I trusted this feeling and by trusting it I was able to act upon it immediately by stopping and giving the patient more anesthetic. This allowed my patients to relax in my chair knowing that I was tuned in with their feelings. They described it as being a caring dentist. They would tell me that no dentist has ever cared for them as much as I have. For the patients, the effect of having a dentist who is intuitive and has enough self-esteem to trust that intuition translates into feeling cared for and feeling safe. Even though I am a natural intuitive, it took me years to build enough self-esteem to trust my intuition and to act on it. Muscle testing is one method that can help strengthen the intuition. Often when the practitioner is muscle testing the patient, they will intuitively know whether the statement being tested is true or false for the patient. When the result of the muscle test confirms that their intuition was correct, they will be able to trust their intuition and improve their intuitive accuracy.

There is a vast difference between the dentist who supports and believes in the holistic model of healthcare and the one who doesn't. Those who are not in alignment with this model will always have difficulty getting their patients to accept and recognize the value of seeing the connection between their emotional stress and their dental health. Patients often don't want to or are not in a place to accept the responsibility required to get healthy. Since the holistic model of healthcare requires the patient to be an integral part of the healing process, without the patient's participation, it is not possible to heal the patient. These patients prefer a quick filling or extraction to fix their immediate problem, and in such cases, conventional dentistry serves them well for a short period of time until the next problem arises.

When a dentist gets clear about the work that they really want to do in their practice and the kind of patients that they want to see (those patients who are willing to do the work), everything will change and they will attract those patients. They will get to not only do the dentistry that they love but they will also get to make a significant difference in their patients' lives by finding the root cause and resolving their dental fears and anxieties.

Prior to discussing the muscle testing methodology and all the steps involved in reducing dental fear and anxiety, it's important to know how these methods were developed. As mentioned earlier, understanding the history of a discovery is as important as the discovery itself because it allows us to have an open mind and an observant heart leaving room for additional discoveries in the field.

Following in the footsteps of Goodheart, applied kinesiology was explored by others to treat psychological problems. While Goodheart discovered a connection among specific muscles, reflexes and meridians, psychiatrist John Diamond and psychologist Roger Callahan independently found correlations with emotions.

John Diamond[14] found correlations between negative emotions and meridians. In other words, certain negative emotions resulting from trauma were found to cause blockage or disruption of energy flow through certain meridians.

Roger Callahan[15] developed a treatment method, which involved attuning psychological problems such as phobias and traumas and then physically tapping on specific acupoints[16] followed by a series of brain exercises while continually thinking about the phobias and traumas. He showed that the phobia or trauma could be eliminated within seconds.

By using applied kinesiology, Callahan developed personal sequences for his patients, and in doing so, he found that certain specific patterns of treatment points were repeatedly emerging for a particular problem, so he went one step further to show the exact order that these points need to be tapped. Callahan named his treatment "Thought Field Therapy (TFT)" and trademarked it as the "Callahan Techniques."[17]

Even though the sequence by which the points were tapped was very much emphasized by Callahan, he maintained that if additional points were included in the tapping sequence, these additional points would not bear any adverse effects on the successful outcome of treatment.

Callahan called these specific tapping sequences "algorithms." Patients who presented with the same problem would all be treated using the particular algorithm that was

---

14   Diamond, *Life Energy*, 1985.

15   Callahan, Roger, *Five Minute Phobia Cure: Dr. Callahan's Treatment for Fears, Phobias and Self-Sabotage.* Blair: Enterprise Publishing Inc., 1985.

16   Gallo, *Energy Psychology,* 2005.

17   Callahan, *Five Minute Phobia*, 1985.

developed for that problem. Dr. Callahan stressed that there were no negative effects because either the algorithm rendered positive results or no results at all.

Acupoints are specific points in the body that are used in Acupuncture (five thousand years old ancient healing system) to stimulate the flow of energy through the insertion of needles, thereby activating the healing network of one's own body. However, Roger Callahan showed that by thinking about a particular psychological concern while tapping on specific acupoints, one is able to influence the body's bioenergy field to eliminate energy imbalances (through elimination of perturbations in the thought field) and in the process, weaken and eliminate negative emotions and the symptoms of psychological distress. In other words, the tapping is theorized to restore the flow of energy in the meridian energy system, thereby defusing the emotional charge that is associated with the negative emotions. He showed that it is not necessary to use needles to stimulate the flow of energy.

In the mid-1990s, Gary Craig (engineer) after studying with Callahan, developed Emotional Freedom Techniques (EFT), which is a derivative of TFT. By realizing that if one taps on all the meridian points, one can successfully eliminate most psychological problems, Craig was determined to make this technique accessible to everyone in the world including, both professionals and the general public. He successfully achieved this by launching an intensive internet campaign to reach people and he taught it successfully by using one basic sequence. In EFT, the process involves the individual to not only imagine but to state out loud a negative emotion or a painful memory while tapping. This imagining and verbalizing the negative emotion or painful memory activates the amygdala, which results in a threat response. The tapping stimulates specific acupoints, which is theorized to then send deactivating signals to the amygdala. This tells the hippocampus to record that now the emotional trigger is safely engaged without a stress response, thus allowing the rewiring and permanent alteration of the neural pathways that initiated the original stress response. Finally, when the stimulus is retriggered, there won't be a limbic arousal and this will become the new pattern.[18] Now that you have learned the history of the discoveries that led to the creation of the methods for dental fear and anxiety reduction, the methodology of muscle testing can be discussed in detail.

In the methods described in this book the muscle that is tested is the middle deltoid muscle. Always ask the person that you are planning to muscle test whether they are comfortable with being touched or if they have any problems with their arm, neck, shoulder, or upper back. If they are comfortable you can proceed with the muscle testing, but if they're not comfortable to be touched for any reason, or are too weak or too young, you can use a surrogate person to test them.

Steps to follow when muscle testing the middle deltoid muscle:

1. Provide the patient with a comfortable chair to sit on with their feet uncrossed and laying comfortably on the floor
2. Ask the patient to bring their dominant arm out directly in front of them and hold it straight and horizontal to the floor

---

18   Feinstein, David, "Acupoint Stimulation in Treating Psychological Disorders: Evidence of Efficacy." *Review of General Psychology* 16 (2012), 364–80. doi:10.1037/a0028602.

3. The hand should be comfortably open and relaxed with the palm facing the floor

4. Position yourself standing to the side of the arm that you are testing

5. Do not stand in front of your patient and do not make eye contact with your patient as doing so can influence their energy and vice versa

6. Let your patient know that you will not be making eye contact with them. Ask them to look ahead but not directly at you

7. Place the first two fingers of your hand on the arm that you're testing right above the wrist

8. You can place your other hand on their opposite shoulder to gain more stability, but if you do this, it is best for them to be standing and not sitting

9. Instruct the patient as follows: "I will ask you to make a statement out loud. Then I will say "hold" and I will gently press down on your arm. Hold means keep your arm steady and strong and resist me pushing your arm down

10. Ask the patient to state their full name. If their name is Jonathan Ronald Smith, they will say: "My name is Jonathan Ronald Smith"

11. Say "Hold" out loud and press gently but firmly downward pressure on their arm that lasts no more than two seconds

12. Their arm will remain straight (locked) and strong because this is a true statement. Even if their arm gives in slightly to the downward pressure and immediately bounces back to its original position, you can consider the muscle as being firm/strong and locked

13. Ask them to state out loud a name other than their real name. In the example presented here you will ask them to state, "My name is Cindy Law" and repeat the muscle test. Because this is a false statement you will see and feel their arm giving away rapidly as the muscle weakens in response to the false statement

To gain experience in muscle testing, perform this exercise on at least thirty people. In addition to stating their name you can ask the person to state something that is very obvious such as the time of the day. If it's 10 a.m. in the morning and sunny you will ask them to state: "It is morning and sunny right now" vs. "It is evening and dark right now." The client will test strong for the first statement (because it is a true statement) and weak for the second statement (because it is a false statement). When muscle testing to test the truth of a statement for your client, often the practitioner finds that they intuitively know the correct answer right before it is confirmed by the muscle testing weak (false statement) or strong (true statement). You will find that the more you listen to your intuition before muscle testing, the more you get to trust your intuition. If you're not naturally intuitive, you might initially dismiss this knowing whisper of your intuition but soon you will trust it more and more.

In cases where your patient is a child and too young to be muscle tested or an elderly patient, it may be necessary to use a surrogate to perform the muscle testing on. To use a surrogate, it is best to gain permission from the patient and in the case where children are the patient, gain permission from the child's legal guardian or parents.

Steps for using a surrogate to test the patient:

1. Muscle test the surrogate to determine a "yes" for a true statement and a "no" for a false statement. This way you can be certain that the surrogate is testable
2. The surrogate needs to make a connection with the patient either by holding the patient's hand or in the case of a young child, holding the patient in their lap
3. Ask the patient to state their full name: "My name is Scott Andrew Smith," then muscle test the surrogate who should test strong
4. Ask the patient to make a false statement such as stating their name to be something other than their true name: "My name is Cindy Law." Test the surrogate who should test weak. If the surrogate does not test weak, repeat steps three and four until the surrogate does test weak. This will confirm that the surrogate has a connection established with the patient
5. Now that the connection between the patient and the surrogate has been established, you can proceed with addressing all the questions to the patient and asking the patient to state the appropriate sentences, but all muscle testing will be done on the surrogate

When a patient cannot be present to be tested, they can authorize someone to act as a substitute for them. This person is referred to as a "proxy." The person who is voluntarily acting as the proxy is in effect agreeing to be tested as if they were the patient, thereby allowing their body to be used to benefit the patient. This can be very beneficial for children who cannot be present for a lengthy session.

In summary, the body tells us if a statement is true (correct statement) by the muscle testing "strong" and if a statement is false (incorrect statement) by the muscle testing "weak."

Sometimes when you're muscle testing your patient to see if they are testable, you'll find that they show no difference between two opposing statements because at some point they have lost polarity, so in effect they have become not testable.

Polarity determines the direction of energy flow in the multi-dimensional aspects of the human energy field. More generally speaking, polarity is the quality in an object that produces opposite magnetic charges. Electrical polarity is either positive or negative and it is a term used to describe the direction that a current flows in an electric circuit. In a direct current (DC) circuit, one pole is always negative while the other pole is positive and the electrons flow in one direction only. In electrical terms, a battery has a positive end and a negative end. The positive end is the giving side (where the energy comes out) or the South Pole, which can be recognized by a protrusion (bump) at its end. The negative end is the receiving side (where energy comes in) or the North Pole with a concave area at its end.

Similarly, human energy fields, although invisible, are like magnetic fields in that they possess a normal direction. When the polarity is correct our energies flow freely. When a person has proper polarity, energy is received from the sun through the top of our head and from the earth through the bottoms of our feet. Therefore, the head and the feet are the North Poles because they receive energy. Energy moves out from the human heart into the world making the heart the South Pole.

When the system loses its polarity it becomes non-polarized, similar to a car engine that is stuck in neutral. Dental patients who have lost their polarity will not be able to make a decision such as whether to follow or not follow your recommendations. To regain polarity and testability do the following:

Restoring testability:

1. Breathe deeply: sometimes patients without realizing stop breathing properly. As a result, they may be lacking oxygen
2. Drink water: Energy flows better in a well-hydrated system
3. Thymus Thump: Smile, think of someone or a pet that you love while thumping on the sternum and saying: "ha ha ha, ha ha ha, ha ha ha"
4. Over-Energy correction (discussed in Chapter 8)
5. Re-schedule or use a surrogate (this is last resort and has been discussed earlier in this chapter)

In this chapter you have learned how to properly muscle test the patient, how to use muscle testing to verify the testability of the patient and to correct loss of testability if needed. Now that you have mastered step one, we can proceed to centering, which is discussed in the next chapter as step two.

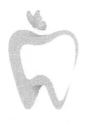

CHAPTER 8:

Centering

To assure the best outcome, the most important aspect of a session begins with making sure that both the patient and the practitioner are fully present inside their body through grounding and their energy system is operating correctly in a naturally flowing pattern. The latter is called "centering," which is the main topic of this chapter.

Eastern healing describes this natural flowing pattern as energies flowing across the center of the body and moving freely within and outside the body in the proper direction. This free and proper flow of energies results in the proper functioning of the system and allows the patient a sense of wholeness, unity, and a firm springboard from which to operate from.

When a person is not grounded and centered, they often describe feeling "spaced out" or "not being with it" or "having their head stuck in the clouds." It is important to make sure the patient is grounded and centered prior to beginning the treatment because if the patient is not properly grounded and centered, the desired outcome of treatment will either be non-existent or short-lived.

The three dimensions or vectors of the human energy field, when centered and in alignment, flow from up to down, front to back, and left to right. By muscle testing the patient, we can determine whether these three vectors are in alignment or not. If muscle testing shows that energy is not flowing correctly in any of these vectors, treatment needs to be initiated to correct the flow of energy so that the energy field can be centered.

Flow of Energy in the Up-Down Vector

In the vertical axis of the body, energy flow is balanced when it freely flows from up to down. When the energy flows in the reverse direction from down to up, the vertical axis of the body is imbalanced because the energy is flowing backward through the system. In Eastern Medicine this is called "counter flow chi."

In regard to our hands, the back of the hand is the North Pole and the receiving side (where energy comes in), whereas the palm of the hand is the South Pole and the giving side where energy comes out. You want to be sure the brain of the patient recognizes up as up and down as down.

If the system's vertical polarity has shifted, then the entire system will run backward. The result in behavior is that the patient will be attracted to what is harmful and repelled by what is helpful. Dental patients will not floss or care for their teeth and gums at home because they are attracted to what is harmful despite your recommendations to the contrary. They will not follow through with keeping appointments that will get them healthy because they are not attracted to health.

1. Diagnose up-down energy imbalance:

Hand-Over-Head Test allows you to assess any vertical polarity problems for your patient. Before you do the following hand-over-head test, first self-test to make sure you don't have a problem with your own polarity. When I'm working with my dentist clients, I always ask them to correct their own polarity problems first before they test their patient.

Muscle test: Ask the patient to place the palm of one hand facing down above but not touching their head. Proper flow is confirmed if muscle tests strong. Then ask the patient to do the same but this time with the palm facing up. Proper flow is confirmed if muscle tests weak. The rationale is that energy comes in through the back of our hands and flows out from the palm of our hands. When the muscle tests strong with the palm facing down, it means energy is flowing properly by exiting the palm of the hand and flowing down. To double check, ask the patient to place their palm facing up to the sky and test them again. The muscle should test weak with the palm facing up showing that this is not proper energy flow and therefore a false statement.

Once the palm down tests strong and the palm up tests weak, the patient is correctly polarized in the vertical axis. In cases where the patient tests backward (weak on palm down and strong on palm up), it also indicates counterclockwise flow instead of clockwise energy flow in the Heart chakra. The following exercise will correct both the up-down energy flow and the counter clockwise flow of energy of the Heart chakra.

2. Correction for up-down energy imbalance:

Heart Massage (Sore Spot Massage) corrects up-down energy imbalance: Ask the patient to place the palm of their right hand on the sore spot above the heart (directly above the nipple between the second and third rib – this neurolymphatic point is where the Lymphatic Vessels empty into the heart cavity) and massage this area in a clockwise circular manner while saying three times self-acceptance statements such as: "I deeply and profoundly accept myself with all my problems and limitations" or "I accept all my feelings about everything." As an option you can add: "I also accept all of my gifts and talents."

It is paramount to our wellbeing to accept our entire selves, including all of the things we don't like about ourselves, such as fear, guilt, anger, gum disease, or cavities to name a few. Whenever we hate something about ourselves our energy becomes trapped in this non-acceptance and we lose our power to change it rendering us feeling helpless. This ultimately adversely affects our well-being. The heart massage is one of the first exercises from Thought Field Therapy that places acceptance into the energy field giving us the power to change for the better (positive change).

3. Longevity of the correction exercise:

This correction (Heart Massage or Sore Spot Massage), usually lasts one hour or less.

"Switching" is a polarity problem that can be created when energy flow through pathways in the body are out of balance mainly due to imbalance of energy flow in the front-back and left-right vectors discussed below. One common way of causing this imbalance is the overuse of one side of the body (such as when carrying a heavy handbag on one arm) causing energy flow between brain hemispheres to be lopsided. Physical signs of switching include lack of physical coordination, bumping into things appearing awkward and clumsy, breaking teeth, or even biting down and injuring the tongue when eating. Switching can be quickly corrected by using the Belly Button Correction (Basic Unswitching Procedure). This is fast and easy but tends to not last as long as the Over-Energy Correction and Collarbone Breathing exercise (both specifically for front-back imbalances) and Cross Crawl and Heart Dyslexia Integration (for L-R imbalances) described below.

Belly Button Correction (Basic Unswitching Procedure) for treatment of front-back and left-right imbalances:

Stimulating the collarbone points corrects energy flow in the front-back vector and stimulating the Conception Vessel (CV) and the Governing Vessel (GV) points help correct energy flow in the left-right vector.

Press, rub, or hook the middle finger into the navel and pull up gently to stimulate the umbilicus and at the same time tap or rub both collarbone points, followed by under the nose (ending of GV), under the lips (end of CV), and Tailbone (optional-beginning of GV). Then repeat the process using the other hand at the navel.

Flow of Energy in the Front-Back Vector

Any imbalance in the front to back axis will adversely affect the proper polarization of the four quadrants of the brain. The right side of the brain is involved in feelings, creativity, and expression whereas the left side is involved with logical reasoning, order, and structural analysis. Each side of the brain consists of two quadrants: frontal and basal, left and right.

These imbalances result in an energy field that is either shifted forward or back, or see-sawing between the two, first swinging forward (producing a racy, hyperactive feeling) and then swinging backward (producing a feeling of crashing from over-expenditure of energy).

1. Diagnose front-back energy imbalance:

The collarbone points (K27) are under each collarbone where it meets the sternum. This is located bilaterally and it represents the end of the Kidney Meridian. Muscle test the strength of the collarbone points (K27) by first placing the fleshy side of the tip of the index and middle fingers (South Pole) on the collar bone points on the left and right sides and then repeating this with the knuckles (North Pole).

The two fingers representing the South Pole will test the basal quadrants while the knuckles (keep the thumb inside the fist) representing the North Pole, will test the frontal quadrants.

All four of these quadrants should muscle test strong. If a quadrant tests weak it means that it is not properly polarized. The neurological result of an improperly polarized quadrant is equivalent to driving a car with a flat tire in that quadrant.

2. Correction for front-back energy imbalance:

Over-Energy Correction: Cross left ankle over the right ankle. Either place the left hand on the right knee and place the right hand on the left knee or stretch the arms out in front of the body with the thumbs facing down; cross the right hand over the left and bring the clasped hands down and rest at the heart. Inhale with the tip of the tongue placed on the roof of the mouth and exhale with the tongue resting on the floor of the mouth. Continue breathing for two minutes with the eyes open or closed. Muscle test the collar bone points again. All four quadrants should test strong.

Usually this exercise needs to be done once per hour for six weeks. After completing the Over-Energy Correction, if any of the four quadrants continue to test weak, do the Collarbone Breathing Exercise below, which is a stronger correction for front-back energy imbalance.

Collarbone Breathing Exercise: Start on the left side by placing the middle and index fingers of the right hand on the left K27 point. Tap the Gamut spot (the web between the ring and middle fingers) while you do the following at least five times in each position. Breathe halfway in, breathe all the way in, breathe even more. Breathe halfway out, breathe all the way out, breathe out even more. Breathe half way in. Place the two fingers of the right hand on the right K27 and do the breathing sequence plus tapping the Gamut spot. Then make a knuckle by hiding the thumb inside the fist of the right hand and place it on the right K27 and repeat the breathing and tapping sequence. Repeat this by placing the knuckles of the right hand on the left side. Then repeat this entire sequence with the left hand. Retest to see if all four quadrants test strong.

Belly Button Correction (the Basic Unswitching Procedure)

3. Longevity of the correction exercise:

The corrections for front-back imbalances usually last one hour or more.

Flow of Energy in the Left-Right Vector

Any imbalance in the flow of energy from left to right will result in improper polarization in this axis and so the energy flow will be switched. Therefore, a person will perceive what they see as backward. It will be challenging to give post-op instructions to this patient or recommend treatment, as neither will be understood properly. This phenomenon is seen in patients with dyslexia. Both of the following corrections need to be repeated three to four times a day for six weeks, as it will take this long to establish proper neural pathways in the brain.

1. Diagnose for left-right energy flow imbalance:

First diagnosis is the Hemispheric Integration: Type a large letter X on a piece of paper. Hold this paper one foot in front of the patient at eye level and ask them to look at the letter X. The muscle when tested should test strong. Then draw two parallel lines so that they fill the entire page. Hold this page one foot in front of the patient and ask the patient to look at the parallel lines. This time the muscle should test weak.

If the patient's muscle does not test strong on X and weak on parallel lines, you need to find out which hemisphere of the brain needs correction. To test the left side of the brain muscle test them while they count. Testing strong means there is proper energy flow in the left side of the brain. To test the right side of the brain muscle test them while they hum a tune. Testing strong means there is proper energy flow on the right side of the brain.

Second diagnosis is the Brain-Heart Coordination: You want to find out if the brain waves (EEG) and the heart waves (EKG) are in synchrony. Repeat the cross-crawl diagnosis while adding a hand over the heart. Muscle should test strong with the letter X and weak with the parallel lines. If these muscle testing results are not achieved, have the patient do the Heart Dyslexia Integration, nickname being Scarecrow Exercise below.

2. Correction for left-right energy imbalance:

i. Cross Crawl Exercise for Hemispheric Integration: Stand comfortably on the floor with arms at your sides. Raise your left knee and bring your right hand forward to tap the left knee. Drop both the arm and the knee back to original place in standing position. Raise the right knee and bring the left hand forward to tap the right knee. Drop both back into place. Repeat this tapping sequence while you do the following: every time you tap the knee count one then two until thirty. So you're tapping the knee left and right and counting at the same time to thirty. Then hum a tune for thirty seconds. Then circle your eyes one way for fifteen seconds and the other way for fifteen seconds. You have the option of circling your eyes while you're counting and humming.

ii. Heart Dyslexia Integration (Scarecrow) Exercise for Brain-Heart Coordination: Similar to a scarecrow or a puppet, raise one elbow up to shoulder height and out to the side of the body. Rotate this upper arm forward so the elbow points straight ahead. Raise the hand and forearm while simultaneously lifting the opposite knee similar to raising the leg like a puppet on a string. Allow both to drop to the floor. Repeat the above using the other arm and leg. Keep repeating this scarecrow exercise first by counting to thirty (say one number with each lift), then by humming for thirty seconds, then circling eyes one way for fifteen seconds and the opposite way for fifteen seconds. Redo the muscle test. If the muscle test is still not right, add the circling of the eyes while you're counting or humming and retest.

3. Longevity of the correction exercise:

Each of the correction exercises above will last three to four hours or more. To establish proper neural pathways in the brain, both of the above corrections need to be repeated three to four times a day for six weeks.

[Note for all three corrections] You can muscle test to find out how long the corrective effect will last and how often the patient needs to do the correction exercises. Muscle test the patient for true/false statements by stating: "This correction will last at least one hour, two hours" etc. and "the correction needs to be done for six weeks once a day, twice a day etc."

Usually for the corrective pattern to hold, the corrective exercises need to be done for six weeks to become permanent.

Finally, muscle test to confirm that the entire system is centered, by asking the patient to say: "My entire system is centered." Muscle should test strong. Then, ask the patient to say: "My entire system is not centered." Muscle should test weak. Once this is achieved continue on to the Anchoring Technique for centering described below. The purpose of this technique is for the patient to be able to recapture his/her center quickly anywhere and at any time.

Anchoring Technique (How to Quickly Recapture Your Patient's Center)

Now that you have a patient who is centered you want to capture this optimal state so that it can be quickly reproduced at any other future time or appointment. To establish the value of this technique, consider the following example. A healthy thirty-year-old patient with a history of dental fear and anxiety is scheduled for a lengthy dental appointment. On her way to the dental office she is rear-ended by another car, which results in her losing her center. By the time she arrives at the dental office she is thirty minutes late and completely frazzled due to the stress of the accident. Fortunately, because she has previously done the work of establishing her center, instead of needing to re-schedule her dental appointment, she guides herself through the Anchoring Technique. This allows her to quickly regain her centering without losing further invaluable time and so her treatment can be started without any further stress.

After the initial appointment when the patient's entire system is centered and confirmed to be centered by muscle testing, the Anchoring Technique is simply accomplished by asking the patient to say the following: "I ask my subconscious mind to program into my system that whenever I touch my thumb and middle finger (do it and take a deep breath) and say/ think the word *center*, my system will center, just like it is right now. This means my polarity is set properly on all parts of the vertical axis, front-back axis, and left-right axis. So, my energy field is centered. *Center*."

To reinforce this programming: For thirty seconds hold the hand position and repeat "*center*" while doing eye movements in a lazy eight pattern, moving up in the center and down on the outsides.

When a client begins their training with me, I usually have them practice these centering exercises with at least ten patients so that they can become confident in performing them correctly. When you begin working with a patient, you can dedicate sixty to ninety minutes to only practicing these centering exercises with them. At the end of this time period your patient will be properly centered and will be able to duplicate this centered state by the Anchoring Technique and so will be able to begin treatment at their next dental appointment without a glitch.

If you only have ninety minutes available for the entire treatment, most of the time you can center the patient by only using the Thymus Thump and/or the Heart Massage (Sore Spot Massage) exercises.

Once your patient is centered you can either begin treatment right away or schedule the patient's next appointment within one week. Remind them that the same pre-appointment instructions apply to the next appointment.

By this point in the treatment, you have accomplished steps one and two. Step one involved using muscle testing to verify the patient's testability and correction when needed. The second step as described in this chapter contained instructions on how to center the patient and then anchor them when in this centered state. Step three, which involves finding and clearing psychological reversals, is discussed in Chapter 10. It is crucial, before continuing on with step three, to discuss meridians (energetic pathways) in the next chapter (Chapter 9) so that the remainder of the steps can be more easily understood and assimilated.

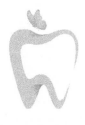

CHAPTER 9:

Meridians

Meridians are pathways in the body that carry information. In Electrical Body,[19] Robert O. Becker explained in detail that meridian pathways carry direct current electrical signals, which travel through perineural cells (cells that form sheaths around axons). Acupuncture points, (sensitive to stimulation) are connected by these meridian pathways. The meridian pathways that are discussed here travel right under the surface of the skin, although there are many that travel deep within the body. Each meridian has a point on the body called the Alarm Point or test point and as you will see these are very useful diagnostically. Meridian energy usually travels at an optimal velocity much like the speed limit set for highways. Any deviations (high or low) from this optimal speed will result in health problems. The phenomenon of Therapy Localization in applied kinesiology

19 Becker, Robert O., and Selden, Gary, *Body Electric: Electromagnetism and the Foundation of Life.* New York: Morrow, 1985.

has shown that by placing your hand on certain specific points on the body, you can identify dysfunctional meridians because they cause a previously strong muscle to test weak. In addition, when a test point is Therapy Localized, the muscle associated with the dysfunction, which had tested weak will immediately test strong. For the TL procedure you can use any muscle to be the indicator muscle if that muscle had tested strong when in the clear. TL in psychological kinesiology involves mental activities such as visualizing, thinking about, or speaking about a certain subject. However, in human functioning there is an intimate dance between the mental, emotional, structural, chemical, postural, and behavioral aspects. If you suspect a dysfunctional condition existing, you can test all the points on the surface of the body to find out which ones are involved in the dysfunctional condition.

Life energy flows into and travels throughout the body within a system of fourteen meridians. There are twelve meridians that run bilaterally in the human body. One runs on the left side of the body and the other runs on the right side tracing the same path as the left meridian. In addition to these, there are two meridians that run up the center of the body. One is called the Conception Vessel, which runs along the center line of the front of the torso ending under the lips and the other is called the Governing Vessel, which runs up the midline of the back of the body, over the head and ends under the nose. Fifty percent of the bilateral meridians are associated with the left hemisphere of the brain. The Alarm points for the left hemisphere meridians are all located on the path of the Conception Vessel. The other half of the bilateral meridians are associated with the right hemisphere with their Alarm points off the body's midline on the lateral sides.

Among the individual meridians there is a circle of energy transfer for the bilateral meridians. This energy transfer travels from the Circulation Sex to Triple Warmer to Gall Bladder to Liver to Lung to Large Intestine to Stomach to Spleen Pancreas to Heart to Small Intestine to Bladder to Kidney and back to Circulation Sex and so on. In this circular pattern for each meridian, the one immediately preceding it is referred to as the "Mother" and the one immediately following it is referred to as the "Son."

Meridians are additionally categorized through a universal classification as being of Yin and Yang polarity. Yin and Yang represent bipolar distinctions such as negative and positive, dark, and light to name a few. In addition, Yin meridians flow on the inside soft surfaces of the body (example: inside of the arms) and the word Yin conveniently rhymes with "in" which helps with recalling. Yang meridians flow on the outer bonier parts of the body (example: the head).

Even if the physical form of an organ or a limb has been surgically removed, chi continues to flow through the associated meridian. Patients who have gone through an amputation have at times reported having sensations in the area of the missing part of the body, which is due to chi continuing to flow through the area of the missing body part.

Amongst the twelve bilateral meridians, six pairs are north-seeking Yin meridians (generally are solid organs) and six pairs are south-seeking Yang meridians. Meridians are paired together based on (1) the functions that they share; for example, the Lung and the Large Intestine are paired together because both organs are involved in elimination, and (2) developing together in the embryo; for example, Bladder and Kidney or Liver and Gall Bladder. The connections that are shared between pairs of meridians last the duration of a lifetime of the individual. Meridians that are in pairs usually consist of one meridian that is north-seeking and one that is south-seeking.

The two regulating meridians, Conception and Governing, are called vessels. The Conception Vessel regulates the six pairs of north-seeking Yin meridians. This vessel represents an energy reservoir for these six Yin meridians: Lung, Spleen/Pancreas, Heart, Kidney, Pericardium, and Liver. The energy in these Yin meridians flows from the earth toward the sky with the arms raised. The Governing Vessel is an energy reservoir responsible for regulating six pairs of south-seeking Yang meridians. These Yang meridians generally collect fluids: Large Intestine, Stomach, Small Intestine, Bladder, Triple Energizer, and Gall Bladder. The energy in the Yang meridians flows from the sky (north) toward the earth (south).

The Lung Meridian receives life energy (chi, qi, prana) through the in-breath and so the Chinese regard this as the prime meridian and believe that the quality of our breathing affects our energy level. The Heart chakra, located in the middle of the seven chakras, regulates the Lung Meridian. Therefore, if the Heart chakra is closed, less life force energy enters and when it's open more enters. Chi flows from the lungs through the twelve organ meridians in the following sequence: Lung, Large Intestine, Stomach, Spleen/Pancreas, Heart, Small Intestine, Bladder, Kidney, Pericardium, Triple Energizer, Gall Bladder, and finally Liver.

Each meridian pair, their associated energy pathways and TFT treatment points (which can be tapped on either side of the body) and their abbreviations are discussed below:

The Lung and the Large Intestine Meridian Pair:

The Lung Meridian (Yin) begins flow beside the shoulder and flows up the raised arm to the thumbnail. Treatment point is thumb (t): base of the thumbnail, radial side (outside).

The Large Intestine Meridian (Yang) begins flow at the index fingernail and ends beside the nose, flowing back down the raised arm. Treatment point is index fingernail (if): base of the index fingernail, radial side.

The Stomach and Spleen Pancreas Meridian Pair:

The Stomach Meridian (Yang) begins flow under the eye (UE) and continues down the body to the second toenail. Treatment point is eye (e): below the center of the eye in the indentation on the intraorbital ridge.

The Spleen Pancreas Meridian (Yin) begins flow at the outside edge of the base of the big toenail and continues up the body to the side of the body under the arm. Treatment point is under arm (ua): eight finger tips width under the armpit.

The Heart and Small Intestine Meridian Pair:

The Heart Meridian (Yin) begins flow at the center of the armpit and continues up the arm to the inside of the little fingernail. Treatment point is little finger (lf): Base of the inside of the little fingernail.

The Small Intestine Meridian (Yang) begins flow on the outer part of the little finger and continues down the arm ending beside the ear. Treatment point is side of hand (sh): outside edge of the palm (side of the hand) where the heartline (the top line at the palm of the hand) intersects the edge/side of the hand.

The Bladder and the Kidney Meridian Pair:

The Bladder Meridian (Yang) begins flow at the inside corner of the eye and continues down the body to the little toenail. Treatment point is eyebrow (eb): beginning of the eyebrow.

The Kidney Meridian (Yin) begins on the sole of the foot and runs up the body to the collarbone. Treatment point is collarbone (c): under the clavicle next to the sternum.

The Pericardium (also called Sex Circulation) and the Triple Energizer Meridian Pair:

The Pericardium (the protective lining around the heart) Meridian begins near the nipple and runs up the arm to the middle fingernail. Treatment point is middle finger (mf): base of the middle fingernail on the thumb side.

The Triple Energizer (also called Triple Warmer/Thyroid) Meridian (Yang) begins on the ring fingernail and runs down the arm to the outside of the eyebrow. Treatment point is back of hand/Gamut Spot (bh): Gamut Spot is at the back of the hand between the fourth and fifth metacarpals.

The Gall Bladder and the Liver Meridian Pair:

The Gall Bladder Meridian (Yang) begins at the outer edge of the eye and runs down the body ending at the fourth toenail. Treatment point is outer eye (oe): outer corner of the eyes, at the same level as the pupils, where the bone above and below the eye meet.

The Liver Meridian (Yin) begins at the inside corner of the base of the big toenail and flows up the body ending on the chest directly below the nipple. Treatment point is rib (r): upper edge of the eighth rib directly below the nipple.

Conception Vessel (singular) begins at a point on the perineum between the anus and the genitalia and runs straight up the front of the torso through the abdomen, chest, and neck and ends at the depression between the lower lip and the chin. Treatment point is under lip (ul): in the depression between the lower lip and the chin.

Governing Vessel (singular) begins at the tip of the coccyx and travels up the back over the head and down to the upper lip and it ends on the center of the gingiva located right above the two central incisors. Treatment point is under nose (un): under the nose directly above the upper lip.

Based on the findings of Diamond,[20] the above treatment points can be traced to the affected meridian and then to the negative feelings that resulted in the disruption of energy flow in that meridian.

Therefore, according to Diamond,[21] the following are examples of the negative emotions that can cause disruption of energy flow in each meridian. Intolerance, disdain, scorn, contempt, and prejudice are associated with causing disruption of energy flow in the Lung Meridian. Guilt disrupts the Large Intestine Meridian. Fear, anxiety, disgust, bitterness, disappointment, greed, hunger, and deprivation disrupt the Stomach Meridian. Fear and anxiety disrupt the Spleen Meridian. Anger disrupts the Heart Meridian. Sadness and sorrow disrupt the Small Intestine Meridian. Trauma, restlessness, impatience, and frustration disrupt the Bladder Meridian. Fear, anxiety, and sexual indecision disrupt the Kidney Meridian. Jealousy, regret, remorse, sexual tension, and stubbornness disrupt

---

20 Diamond, *Life Energy,* 1985.
21 Ibid.

the Pericardium Meridian. Depression, despair, heaviness, grief, hopelessness, despondency, and loneliness disrupt the Triple Energizer Meridian. Rage, fury, wrath, frustration, and indecision disrupt the Gall Bladder Meridian. Unhappiness disrupts the Liver Meridian. Shame disrupts the Conception Vessel. Lastly, embarrassment, inferiority and powerlessness disrupt the energy flow in the Governing Vessel. For a complete list of negative emotions refer to John Diamond's book Life Energy.

The results of a study that I did in 2013, *examining the effects of customized meridian treatments for dental anxiety*, showed that sixty-seven percent of the individuals with dental fear and anxiety identified a combination of EB, SE and UE acupressure points as treatment points for dental anxiety. These findings indicated disruption of energy flow in the Bladder, Gall Bladder, and the Stomach Meridians.

The same study showed eyebrow point to be the treatment point most commonly identified on all the participants. This is the treatment point for the Bladder Meridian. Amongst the negative emotions that ride on the Bladder Meridian are trauma, restlessness, impatience, and frustration. Therefore, it can be concluded that all the participants were suffering from trauma in relation to their past dental experiences or one or more traumatic non-dentistry related experience(s). This explains why so many dental patients exhibit the following behaviors while sitting in the dental chair: (1) being fidgety, (2) looking at their watch constantly asking, "Are you done yet?" (3) making you feel as though you're the one who is slow, and (4) experience frustration regardless of how hard you try to make their appointment pleasant. It's enough to treat one patient like this and you're drained for the rest of your day.

For eighty-three percent of the subjects, the eyebrow and the outer eye were identified as treatment points. These are associated with disruption of energy flow in the Bladder and Gall Bladder Meridians. If these numbers represent the patients in your practice, it is possible that eighty-three percent of your patients experience trauma, restlessness, impatience, wrath, rage, fury, frustration, and indecision.

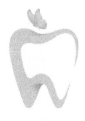

CHAPTER 10:

When Wanting and Doing Are Complete Opposites

A psychological reversal can be described as an inner conflict where one part of the person wants the goal and another part, for various reasons, doesn't want it. An example of a psychological reversal is the lung cancer patient who knows that if he stops smoking, he can survive, but despite declaring that he wants to live, he continues to smoke. In step three, as described in this chapter, you may discover the presence of one or many psychological reversals. When a psychological reversal is uncovered it has to be treated before assessing whether another one is present or not. This needs to be continued until all psychological reversals are corrected before proceeding to the next step (step four) of finding which meridian pathways have disrupted energy flow.

Usually limiting beliefs create inner conflicts. Using the example of the person who burned his hand on the stove as a child, the limiting belief that can result in adulthood was "stoves and kitchens are not safe." This individual can then have an inner conflict around safety, because he wants to have a house with a beautiful kitchen so that he and his family can enjoy homemade meals, but he finds something wrong with every house that has a kitchen with a stove. Therefore, this person cannot move forward with purchasing a house until the Psychological Reversal of Safety (it's safe to be over this problem vs. it's not safe to be over this problem) is treated. Once this is treated, he may or may not have other reversals such as Possibility (it's possible to be over this problem vs. it's not possible to be over this problem) as an example.

The reversal categories around which limiting beliefs form inner conflicts are as follows: Live/Die, Misery (Happiness/ Suffering), Want, Possibility, Deserving, Benefit, Safety for Self, Safety for Others, Future/Never, Willingness/Motivation, Deprivation, Vengeance, Identity, Permission, and Mini.

Diagnosis for Reversals:

To diagnose whether a reversal is present or not, first muscle test the generic statement: "I have no objection to being over this issue" followed by muscle testing the opposing statement: "I have at least one objection to being over this issue." It's important to always muscle test both the generic statement and the opposing statement to assure certainty. If the first statement (I have no objection to being over this issue) muscle tests strong, it means there is no reversal present. If this is true, the opposing statement (I have at least one objection to being over this issue) will muscle test weak. When the muscle test shows that the patient has no objections, meaning that no reversals are present, continue on to step four to find which meridians have disrupted energy flow.

Diagnosis and Correction of Reversals:

If the patient muscle tests weak for having no objection and strong for having at least one objection, meaning there is a reversal present, the next step is to find out which category of reversal is responsible for blocking the path to healing.

When testing to see which reversal is present, first muscle test one category's diagnostic statement and then muscle test that category's opposing limiting belief statement. As an example, if you start with the Want category of reversal, the diagnostic statement, "I want to be over this problem" is muscle tested first and then the opposing statement/limiting belief "I want to keep this problem" is muscle tested second.

If the muscle tests strong on the diagnostic statement ("I want to be over this problem") and weak on the opposing/ limiting belief statement ("I want to keep this problem"), the "Want" flavor of reversal does not exist. Continue on and test the next category of reversal until you find the reversal that is present.

Using the Want category of reversal as an example, when a particular flavor of reversal is present, the muscle will test weak for the diagnostic statement ("I want to be over this problem"), and strong on the opposing limiting belief statement ("I want to keep this problem").

Once you identify the reversal, treat that reversal before checking for any additional reversals. To treat the reversal, you need to first find the spot where the reversal is hiding. To illustrate, let's use the Want reversal as an example again. Ask the patient to place two fingers (usually the index finger and middle finger) of one hand on the most commonly found hiding spot for this reversal (customize if a common hiding spot has not been found), which for the Want reversal is the "sore spot" point and then muscle test while repeating the diagnostic statement for the reversal ("I want to be over this problem"). If muscle tests strong then this is the hiding point for this reversal. To treat this reversal, ask the patient to tap this point while stating out loud the corresponding treatment statement several times ("I totally love and accept myself even though I have this problem or I totally love and accept myself even though a part of me wants to keep this problem").

Once you have treated the location of that flavor of reversal, you want to be sure that this treatment was sufficient to eliminate the reversal by retesting the diagnostic statement, "I want to be over this problem" without touching a point. If the muscle tests strong you have successfully treated that reversal. If it tests weak, proceed to find the next point that the reversal may be hiding and repeat the process (touch a point and state the diagnostic statement for the reversal – if muscle tests strong treat that point). Usually clearing only one point can treat a reversal, but sometimes many points have to be cleared before the reversal is truly treated.

Now go back and muscle test the original statement of "I have no objection to solving this problem" and "I have at least one objection …" without touching a point. If there is no objection the muscle will test strong on the first statement and weak on the second statement. This means that there are no more reversals present. If the opposite happens it means there is another reversal present and so proceed as before to finding which category is present and treat it. If there are no reversals present proceed to the next step, which is finding which meridian pathways have disrupted energy flow.

After treating all the reversals, as you proceed to treat the disrupted energy flow through the meridians, you might achieve some progress but find that the SUD (subjective unit of distress) level does not decrease and remains stuck somewhere above level two. If this happens, it means that another psychological reversal has shown itself, preventing change in the condition being treated and interfering with further progress. Go back and find which flavor it is and treat it before proceeding further.

Tapping Instructions for Your Patient:

Instruct your patient to tap with the fingertips of two fingers (usually the index and middle fingers). Tapping should be done continuously without heavy pressure; you don't want to tap so hard that it ends up hurting. At the same time that your patient is tapping they need to be breathing as well. They may need to be reminded to breathe, as some people tend to forget to breathe when they tap. Tapping engages the impulses that run through the nerve cells and the energetic system, thereby correcting the flow of energy that has been disrupted.

Customizing a Reversal Correction Point:

If you find that the hiding place for the reversal is not the commonly found point it is very easy to find (customize) where the reversal is truly hiding. The points that you can muscle test for are: Crown chakra, Third Eye chakra, Under nose, Under lip, Heart chakra, Side of hand, Back of hand, and Middle fingernail.

Ask the patient to place two fingers of one hand on one point (start with the crown chakra point and only touch the point –

do not tap) while asking your patient to repeat the diagnostic statement for that reversal. As an example: for the Want reversal the diagnostic statement is "I want to be over this problem." Proceed to muscle test the free arm. If the muscle tests strong you have found the hiding place of the reversal (in this example Want reversal is hiding on the crown chakra treatment point) and if it tests weak this is not the hiding place and you move on to test the next spot.

In my 2013 study mentioned earlier in Chapter 9, the following reversals were found to be present in the patients participating in the study: Safety, Motivation/Willingness, Permission, Misery/Happiness, Benefit, Identity, Possibility, Vengeance, Never/Future, and Mini.

For the above reversals, Table 1 below, lists the diagnostic statements, the opposing limiting beliefs, the most common correction points, and the treatment statements. Remember that when you're finding where the reversal is hiding, request patient to place two fingers on the point and repeat out loud the diagnostic statement before you muscle test the opposing arm. When you have found the treatment point for the reversal and you're treating/clearing the reversal, request patient to tap on the point while repeating out loud, the treatment statement.

Reversal	Diagnostic Statement	Limiting Belief	Common Correction Point	Treatment Statement
Safety (self)	It's safe for me to be over this problem	It's not safe for me to be over this problem	Side of Hand	I totally accept myself even if getting over this problem does not feel safe for me
Motivation / Willingness	I am willing to be over this problem	I am not willing to be over this problem	Forehead (Third eye chakra)	I totally accept myself even if I don't do what is necessary to get over this problem
Permission	I will allow myself to get over this problem	I will not allow myself to get over this problem	Customize: Test all the points to find the right one	I totally accept myself even if I will not allow myself to get over this problem.
Misery / Happiness	I want to be happy	I want to be miserable	Customize	Even if I was taught that I should be miserable, maybe I have suffered enough
Benefit	Getting over this problem will be good for me (or others)	Getting over this problem will not be good for me (or others)	Customize	I totally accept myself even if getting over this problem will not be good for me (or others)
Identity	I know who I am if I get over this problem	I won't know who I am if I get over this problem	Side of Hand	Even if I will not know who I am, if I get over this problem, I love and accept myself
Possibility	It is possible to be over this problem	It is not possible to be over this problem	Side of Hand	I totally accept myself even if getting over this problem is not possible
Vengeance	If I get over this problem someone else will have gotten away with hurting me	I have no need for vengeance	Crown Chakra or Under the Lip	Even if part of me wants vengeance more than I want my own healing I totally accept myself
Future / Never	I will be over this problem	I will never be over this problem	Under the Nose	I totally accept myself even if I never get over this problem
Mini	I want to be completely over this problem	I want to keep some of this problem	Side of Hand	I totally accept myself whether or not I ever completely get over this problem

Summary of the Steps for Reversal Diagnosis:

1. Muscle test the two generic statements: "I have no objection to being over this problem" vs. "I have at least one objection to being over this problem."

2. If the muscle tests strong on the first statement (no objection) and weak on the second statement (having a least one objection), you are done with reversals and you can proceed with treating the meridian pathways that have disrupted flow.

3. If the muscle tests weak on the first statement (no objection) and strong on the second statement (having at least one objection) it means patient has at least one objection to being over this problem. Find which flavor of reversal is present.

4. Muscle test to find which category of reversal is present: Choose one reversal category and muscle test to find out if the muscle tests strong on the diagnostic statement or the opposing limiting belief statement. If muscle tests strong for the diagnostic statement (example: I want to be over this problem) and weak to the second statement (I want to keep this problem), your patient does not have this reversal. If muscle tests weak for the diagnostic statement (I want to be over this problem) and strong for the limiting belief statement (I want to keep this problem), you have found the reversal flavor.

5. Find the treatment point for this reversal: patient touches the point while stating out loud the diagnostic statement and you muscle test their opposing arm. If muscle tests strong then that is the point where the reversal is hiding.

6. Treat the point by patient tapping the point (or massaging in the case of the heart), stating out load the treatment statement several times.

7. Retest the diagnostic statement without touching the point. If the muscle tests strong return to step one on this list. If the muscle tests weak, find and treat the next point that tests strong.

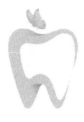

CHAPTER 11:

Creating a Customized Meridian Sequence – from Blockage to Free Flow

You've done the work of learning how to muscle test, how to center your patient, how to find and treat psychological reversals, and how to find and treat meridian pathways with disrupted energy flow. Now you are ready to put it all together in order to create a customized meridian sequence of tapping that is specific for your patient suffering from dental fear and anxiety.

As discussed earlier, once you determine that a patient has fears and anxieties around dental treatment, ask them if they are willing to reduce these negative feelings through an innovative energy-based method. Each time you help a patient go through this journey, ask them to write about their experience and how this protocol helped them. Once you have their permission to share, you can share the benefits they gained with other patients who can benefit from this protocol. Doing so can prove to be very empowering for your patients as they will be assured that they're not the only ones with this problem.

Provide your patient with a brief overview and ask whether they have any reservations around being touched on their arm, shoulders, and upper back. Ask them to read and sign an informed consent prior to starting the treatment.

How to Introduce Your Patient to Energy-Based Methods:

Since acupuncture is now highly accepted in the medical system, you can tell your patients that this is similar to acupuncture but without needles. For a more elaborate explanation, it's always best understood if the method is described within a story using examples of patients who have undergone treatment (confidentiality needs to be preserved, of course.) The following is a generic example:

"I helped a patient who had terrible fears around dental treatment. She was scared the night before and during her appointment; so much so that I couldn't do the excellent dentistry that I'm trained to do. She had cavities and gum disease and she knew that if she didn't get the care that she needed she would lose all her teeth. When we started, she was very ambivalent but within two sessions we found the original source of her fear, which actually had nothing to do with dentistry. When she was a child her brother and his friends who were much older, played games where they would come from behind and scare her unexpectedly in the dark by shining the light of multiple flashlights in her eyes and then they would proceed to tickle her while laughing at her until she became hysterical and would end up screaming and terrified.

She continually asked her brother and his friends to stop doing this and they agreed only until the next opportunity presented itself, so in effect, even though they said they would stop, they never did. Her parents told her to lighten up and not be so sensitive. She was told to "just play the game." To everyone else it was an innocent game but to her it was torture and a nightmare. The trauma of this experience led her to believe that people who are in a position to protect you always betray your trust. Based on her experience it was not safe for her to trust people. She felt that things are never as they appear (being tickled seems innocent and fun but it's not). She believed that life is not safe, her feelings and needs are not important, people who are supposed to take care of her let her down and never keep their promises and no one ever listens to her. So, it was no wonder that every time she was in a dental chair with the overhead light shining on her face knowing that she had to stay still she was triggered to relive all the negative emotions that she felt as a child.

This traumatic experience had resulted in her brain being programmed to send out electrical signals that led to emotions such as anxiety, depression, anger, and disappointment to name a few. Such emotions and behaviors are not appropriate or helpful when she encounters a different situation that is meant to help her such as when sitting in the dental chair to receive much needed dental care.

In energy psychology, this problem is approached by working directly with the energies that maintain the pattern of how your brain responds when faced with a triggering experience. This is done by first collecting information about how the energies in the body are affected by this problem. The energy disturbances are identified and then corrected through a variety of methods that will be discussed as we proceed. Going back to the example of this patient every time she was faced with laying down in a dental chair and being anesthetized, certain parts of her brain became over stimulated, flooding her with negative emotions that got in the way of obtaining much needed dental care. To alter the dysfunctional response in her brain, she was asked to think about the situation while touching/tapping certain trigger points (same points that are used in acupuncture where needles are placed to achieve the desired effect) on her body. Doing this retrained her body and brain to not overreact the next time she sat in a dental chair and was reminded of that negative experience in her childhood. Throughout this method we use a simple method of muscle testing, which involves placing a small amount of pressure on the middle deltoid muscle to find out how your body's energies are involved with your problem. It is a well-known fact in kinesiology that muscles and nerves work together, which is why a negative thought/emotion can weaken the muscle and a positive thought/emotion has the effect of strengthening the muscle. This does not mean that the muscle becomes weak at these times but more accurately the flow of electricity moving through the nerves is momentarily interrupted resulting in the muscle not being able to operate at its best. I'll be asking you to hold your arm out straight in front of you and I'll instruct you to think about the problem that you want help with while I check your muscle for firmness. I will also ask you to do other things like moving your eyes in different directions in order to integrate the treatment. The final goal is for you to be able to experience your dental treatments with ease and comfort instead of fear and anxiety. Does this resonate with what you want as well?"

I have never encountered a patient who did not eagerly accept this treatment.

Interview your patient to assess their level of fear and anxiety regarding dental treatment. This can be achieved by having an informal discussion with your patient by asking them to name all of the things that they find fearful and anxiety inducing around dental treatment. Allow them to express this verbally and write these triggers down on a piece of paper, as you will need to recount them later.

Since they are present in your office, they are already thinking about their fears so you don't need to recreate anything for them, which saves considerable time. Be sure to wear whatever you usually wear when treating patients. If you usually wear a white coat over your scrubs, then wear that because you want to present the patient with the exact scenario that they will be faced with when sitting in a dental chair ready to receive treatment from you.

Ask the patient to subjectively rate his/her level of fear and anxieties on a scale of zero to ten with zero being no fear/anxiety (no distress) and ten being the most severe form of fear/anxiety (extreme distress). This measurement system, called the Subjective Unit of Disturbance or Distress (SUD) allows you to assess how strong an emotional signal is in your patient's thought field. In other words, the SUD scale signifies the amount of distress that the problem creates for your patient. During the entire treatment you will be keeping record of their SUD levels by writing them down so that you can track your patient's progress.

Ask the patient if they are granting you permission to treat this problem. When they verbally state their agreement, I recommend asking them to state their full names three times out loud. Doing so will bring them both physically and energetically into the present moment. Assess the correctness of their response by testing the deltoid muscle. If this is the first time you're muscle testing the patient begin the muscle testing by asking the patient to state their full name ("My name is Andrea Smith") and muscle test and then ask them to state their name falsely ("My name is Roger Tollin") and muscle test. This way you will get a feel for how the muscle feels when testing strong and weak. Then you can muscle test them for permission to treat this problem ("I grant full permission to Dr. Kat to treat my fear and anxiety surrounding dental treatment"). If the muscle tests strong you have permission and if the muscle tests weak you don't have permission. Always test the opposing statement as well ("I do not grant full permission to Dr. Kat to treat my fear and anxiety around dental treatment"). This should test weak if the patient is granting you permission. You get the idea that a true statement will always test strong and a false statement will test weak.

After gaining permission to proceed, test the patient on their state of centeredness based on the three vectors of energy (up to down, front to back and left to right). If you have already worked with this patient on centering merely ask them to center by touching their thumb and middle fingers together and saying out loud: "Center." If you have not worked with this patient before, or even if you have, in the presence of polarity imbalances/shifts, which can occur simply by getting stuck in traffic, correct these by asking them to do the Thymus Thump and the Heart Massage exercises for becoming centered.

To recap, when energy flow is switched, instead of the energy entering through the head, travelling to the heart, and exiting from the heart into the world, its direction is reversed. In a reversed state, something that should help the person deal with their problem will make them feel worse, and something that is bad for the person will make them feel good. Therefore, if you proceed with treatment while a patient's energy flow is switched you will not get correct information.

Thymus Thump is performed by asking the patient to smile, think of someone they love, and with a closed fist, thump on the sternum and say, "Ha ha ha, ha ha ha, and ha ha ha."

The Heart Massage is performed by asking the patient to place the palm of the right hand over the heart and massage clockwise in a circle on the sore spot between the second and third ribs, directly above the nipple, while repeating three times, "I deeply and profoundly accept myself with all my problems and limitations."

After doing these exercises, be sure to muscle test your patient to assess whether they are centered enough to give accurate information.

Usually these exercises correct any imbalances but if they don't, go back and do all the exercises in Chapter 8 to gain adequate centeredness so that it can be confirmed by muscle testing.

The next step is to find out if there are any psychological reversals present. Psychological reversals were described in detail in Chapter 10 as an inner conflict where one part of the person wants the goal and another part doesn't want it for various reasons. An example of psychological reversal is the dental patient with periodontal disease who knows that if she completes the recommended treatment and stays diligent about her home care, she will be able to keep her teeth. But despite declaring that she wants to keep her teeth, she continues to not complete the recommended treatment and does not comply with homecare instructions.

A psychological reversal feels like you're stuck in quicksand. The more you try to get out of it the more you sink into it. When you realize a problem exists that requires change, all your efforts to produce that change lead to the exact opposite of the desired result. It's frustrating to even write about it – so I hope you can see the importance of clearing them.

When a psychological reversal is uncovered it needs to be treated before assessing whether another is present or not. Continue with this protocol until all psychological reversals are corrected as confirmed by muscle testing the patient.

At this point, ask the patient to think about and connect to the list of triggers as reported by them earlier while you read them out loud. Proceed with muscle testing the patient. If the muscle tests strong, it means the problem is resolved and you can take them through the Eye Roll step (discussed at the end of this chapter). If the muscle tests weak, it means you need to find which meridian is disrupted. This starts the process of creating the customized meridians.

To find out which meridian pathways have disrupted energy flow, ask your patient to think about the problem (always better to read out loud the list of fears and anxieties back to them) while placing two fingers of one hand on the treatment point of each meridian starting with the inner eyebrow. If the muscle tests strong for the meridian that is being touched, it means there is disruption of energy flow in this meridian and it needs to be treated. You can then treat this meridian by asking your patient to tap on this treatment point while thinking about the problem and breathing.

The next step is to find out whether additional meridians are involved or not. This can be achieved by stating the problem out loud, and muscle testing. If the muscle tests weak, it means additional meridians are involved. Ask your patient to touch the treatment point for the next meridian while thinking about the problem and muscle testing. If the muscle tests strong, treat that point by asking your patient to think about the problem while tapping and breathing. Continue this protocol of finding the sequence of all the meridians affected by the problem until the muscle tests strong when your patient thinks about the problem. Be sure to record the sequence of the meridians as they are identified and treated for energy flow disruptions.

To summarize, at this point all the reversals are cleared, any meridians with disrupted energy flow have been treated, and this is confirmed by muscle testing strong while your patient thinks about the problem. Therefore, the treatment sequence is finished.

Ask your patient to subjectively rate their SUD level. If this number is two or less, you can proceed forward. If it is more than two, either a psychological reversal has emerged that requires clearing or another meridian has disrupted flow and needs to be treated. Sometimes, it's as simple as just asking your patient if there is something else that is bothering them that they have not talked about. At this stage patients often know of an additional negative feeling that has come into their awareness. If they know and can tell you what it is, you can muscle test them on that particular trigger and you'll find that they will test weak, confirming that there is additional work to do. An example of this can be seen in participant three in Chapter 13.

First determine if there is a psychological reversal present by muscle testing "I have no objection to be over this problem" and "I have at least one objection to being over this problem." If a psychological reversal is present, find out which flavor it is and clear it. If none is present, determine if a meridian needs to be treated by placing two fingers on each meridian point, asking the patient to think about the problem and muscle testing. If muscle tests strong treat that meridian and include this meridian in the sequence of tapping.

In order for your patient to integrate the treatment tapping sequence, ask him/her to perform the 9-Gamut Treatment and sandwich this with another round of tapping. The 9-Gamut Treatment is comprised of nine rapid treatments performed while tapping the Gamut Spot." This spot is located on the back of the hand in the valley that exists between the knuckles of the ring finger and the little finger.

The 9-Gamut Treatment sequence: Ask your patient to tap the Gamut Spot of one hand while following these steps: (i) close eyes, (ii) open eyes, (iii) move eyes down to one side, (iv) move eyes down to the other side, (v) rotate eyes one full circle in one direction, (vi) rotate eyes one full circle in the opposite direction, switch hands and tap the Gamut Spot of the other hand while (vii) humming a tune for five seconds, (viii) counting from one to five and (ix) humming a tune again for five seconds.

The 9-Gamut Treatment integrates the treatment tapping sequence by coordinating and balancing both brain hemispheres while the patient is attuning to the problem. Since the right hemisphere of the brain (involves creativity, art, and expression such as music and humming) affects the left side of the body and the left hemisphere (involves logic, planning, and mathematics such as counting) affects the right side of the body, concurrently looking down to the lower right and counting activates the left hemisphere and vice versa, looking down to the lower left and humming activates the right hemisphere.

Next step is to ask your patient to repeat tapping the customized treatment sequence.

One more time state out loud the list of triggers for the problem and muscle test. If muscle tests weak it means a deeper level of the problem has revealed itself and needs treatment. Go back to finding which reversal is present and clear it.

Repeat the problem out loud and ask your patient to focus on the problem again. Ask them to rate their SUD. Then proceed to muscle test to confirm that your patient is testing strong while thinking about the problem. If they test strong, take them through the Eye Roll.

The floor-to-ceiling Eye Roll is usually the final treatment performed after the earlier steps have resulted in improvements in the SUD score down to a one or two. The Eye Roll will solidify this improvement to either strengthen the one rating or reduce the rating of two to a one.[22] The Eye Roll is done by tapping on the Gamut Spot of one hand while closing the eyes, opening the eyes, and then slowly rolling the eyes from the floor up to the ceiling.

Record the final SUD level.

---

22 Callahan, Roger, and Trubo, Richard, *Tapping the Healer Within: Using Thought-Field Therapy to Instantly Conquer Your Fears, Anxieties, and Emotional Distress.* New York: McGraw Hill Professional, 2001.

CHAPTER 12:

The Story and the Homework

Based on the meridian tapping sequence that you found, create a story to help your patient understand the origin of the problem and why they have a problem. Understanding can often create the needed space for self-compassion. When a person endures a difficult experience, this gets stored in their memory bank and causes disruption of energy flow in the associated meridian. At any future moment this negative experience (stored in their memory) can become activated exposing the negative thoughts and emotions. As an example, if your patient has had a bad drowning experience, they will have a fear of being immersed or stepping into a body of water. This fear is not present when they call your office to make an appointment. However, once they sit in your dental chair and feel the water being squirted in their mouth along with the continuous spray of water from your high-speed drill, that fear (target problem) will be activated. This is one way of creating a problem state. Another way is to create the state of the drowning experience by having the patient think about it. For the energy treatment to effectively impact the target problem, that problem has to be activated in your patient's energy system.[23]

The customized meridian treatment sequence consists of the meridians with disrupted energy flow that you sequentially uncover. In this sequence, the original core meridian that was affected due to the original trauma is always the last meridian that is uncovered. When you review the meaning of the customization with your patient you will review the customized meridian treatment sequence in reverse. By creating a story you can help your patient understand the association between the disrupted meridian and the negative feelings that it causes.

As an example, if the core meridian is the Spleen (located under the arm), you know that disruptions in flow of energy in the Spleen Meridian cause negative feelings of "fear" and "realistic anxiety about the future." So, you can explain this to your patient by creating a story that makes sense to them such as: "Something happened to you in your life which caused you to feel very fearful and this also led you to have realistic anxieties about your future." Then you will explain the next to the last meridian and so on. Further examples are given in the case studies in Chapter 13.

For the effect of the treatment sequence to become permanent you will need to send the patient home with homework. By muscle testing you can discover the duration of self-treatment that is required for permanence. This can be expressed in the form of the number of times per day to the number of months or years.

---

23 Feinstein, David, *Energy Psychology Interactive: Rapid Interventions for Lasting Change.* Ashland: Innersource, 2004.

To discover how many times your patient needs to tap the customized meridian sequence per day, you can start with muscle-testing your patient with questions such as these: "I need to tap three times or less per day" and the opposing statement: "I need to tap four times or more per day." If the muscle tests strong for the first statement and weak for the second statement, to narrow it down further, muscle test the statement: "I need to tap three times per day" and "I need to tap twice or less per day." Once you have determined the number of times per day, follow the same methodology to muscle test the number of weeks.

Provide the following information to the patient to take home. I always recommend to my clients to record this in the patient's chart as well: The story, the sequence and location of the treatment points, the number of times per day for the number of weeks required to achieve permanence.

When this patient returns for dental treatment you will already know the tapping sequence. If for any reason they need to tap to alleviate fear and anxiety before or during their appointment, this information can be quickly accessed. Prior to their appointment, during the same call that is made to remind them of their appointment, your front office staff can also remind them to tap the night before and one hour before their appointment time in addition to keeping their regular tapping schedule. Instead of referring to this as "an appointment reminder call" you can call it "appointment comfort call" or "appointment care call."

CHAPTER 13:

Case Studies

Originally when I started my research in 2013, I was eager to find out whether creating customized meridian treatments would successfully alleviate dental fear and anxiety or not. I had no idea if it was going to work and if it did work, I had no idea to what degree it would work. In addition, even if it did work, I didn't know if the results would last for any length of time.

The first exercise I did was to muscle test anyone who would agree to be muscle tested. Within one hour I found twenty people who agreed to be tested. Next, I asked people if I could muscle test to find out whether their energetic system was balanced and properly functioning, and if it wasn't, I could recommend exercises to achieve proper flow of energy. Again, everyone I asked responded with a "yes, of course." I then checked for psychological reversals and learned how to clear those. Each practice client allowed me to become more proficient until I was ready to create customized meridian treatment sequences. Each time I asked someone if they wanted to participate in my study, they would openly welcome the participation. Not only did they welcome it, but also, they believed I was offering them a gift. What they didn't know was that with their agreement to participate, I was the one receiving the gift.

Below, I have provided examples of sessions to help in understanding different scenarios. The identity of the six participants has been changed to protect their privacy. All participants rated the level of their dental fear and anxiety prior to the session to be above six. On average the duration of each session was ninety minutes except one that ran two and a half hours. My hope is that sharing these stories will help you understand how dental fear and anxiety can originate from so many different types of experiences in an individual's life and how effectively these methods alleviate the accompanying negative feelings. A customized treatment is required because every individual's experience is different and so are the negative feelings that arise from those experiences. One shoe does not fit all. Every individual requires their own unique sequence of meridian tapping treatment, which is based on so many factors including their individual experience, how that experience negatively impacted them, which negative beliefs and psychological reversals were formed, and which meridians were disrupted.

Participant One

Participant One is a thirty-five-year-old male. Initially he rated his SUD at being ten. During the initial interview he mentioned that he had severe fear and anxiety about the following: Sound of the drill, not getting completely numb, anticipating pain and bad news, feeling claustrophobic, being confined in the chair, neck hurting, not being able to move around at will, mouth being open, feeling mouth to be dry, and not being able to close the mouth for rest or to swallow at will.

I have provided dental treatment to this individual and the following are my observations of his behavior changing when he finds out that he needs dental treatment. As soon as I recommend treatment and he realizes that he has to make an appointment, he instantly changes from being an extrovert to an introvert (becomes very quiet and reserved). He rapidly enters a state of depression and anxiety as though a veil of darkness takes over his life energy and covers him like a thick impervious blanket.

When he arrives for his appointment and is seated in the dental chair, he becomes visibly uncomfortable and shows this by moving around continuously in a wiggling motion and complains of neck, shoulder, and back pain. He immediately asks for plenty of anesthetic and is very verbal about his fear of not being able to get completely numb. When patients experience such a high level of fear and anxiety, they do require more anesthetic than usual and once numb, they lose the state of numbness much more quickly than a patient without anxiety. He tries to delay treatment by constantly attempting to speak and ask questions. He visibly becomes covered in beads of sweat across his face, hairline, and neck. He also attempts to dictate treatment by choosing an alternate, less ideal treatment requiring less time to complete, despite knowing it is not the treatment he has chosen at his last visit.

After determining that he was centered on all three vectors of energy, I proceeded to muscle test to see if there were any psychological reversals present. Muscle testing showed that he did have at least one objection to getting over the problem of his dental anxiety by his muscle testing strong and the opposing statement of having no objection, testing weak.

To uncover which flavor of psychological reversal was present, the diagnostic statement of each flavor of reversal was stated while muscle testing. The first psychological reversal that was uncovered was Safety (diagnostic statement: "It is safe for me to be over this problem"). To find out which area was the best area for clearing this reversal, he was asked to place two fingers on his crown chakra first, while repeating the diagnostic statement ("It is safe for me to be over this problem"). His muscle tested strong indicating that the crown chakra was the best area to treat this reversal. After tapping on the crown chakra while repeating the treatment statement ("I totally accept myself even though getting over this problem does not feel safe to me"), it became evident that he needed an additional point of treatment residing on the third eye chakra to clear the reversal. The second psychological reversal that was uncovered was Motivation which cleared after tapping the third eye chakra, while repeating the treatment statement ("I totally accept myself even if I don't do what is necessary to get over this problem"). The third psychological reversal that was uncovered was Permission which cleared after tapping on the crown chakra and then under the nose while repeating the treatment statement ("I totally accept myself even if I will not allow myself to get over this problem"). The fourth psychological reversal that was uncovered was the Mini which was cleared after tapping the crown chakra, while repeating the treatment statement ("I totally accept myself whether or not I ever get completely over this problem"). At this point, his muscle testing indicated having no other objections to getting over this problem by testing strong and testing weak to the opposing statement of having at least one objection. It was concluded that there were no other reversals present.

The participant was asked to rate his SUD level and he reported his SUD at a level of seven. He was asked to think about all aspects of his dental fear and anxiety and his muscle tested weak. I proceeded to create a customized meridian treatment sequence for him. This sequence first involved the inner eyebrow and then under the nose. I asked him to think about his dental anxiety and muscle tested him again. He tested strong. I took him through the 9-Gamut Treatment and repeated the sequence of tapping. I muscle tested him again while he thought about his dental anxieties and he tested weak. He reported his SUD level was five.

I went back to checking for psychological reversals again. His muscle testing showed he had at least one more objection to being over this problem. The fifth reversal that was uncovered was Misery. This was cleared after tapping the third eye chakra. The sixth reversal that was uncovered was Benefit. This reversal was cleared after tapping the crown chakra. The seventh reversal that was uncovered was Identity. This reversal was cleared after tapping the third eye chakra. Participant tested strong when muscle tested for "I have no objection to being over this problem" and tested weak when muscle tested for "I have at least one objection to being over this problem." This confirmed that he no longer had any reversals present. He reported his SUD level at four.

I asked him to think about his dental anxiety and he muscle tested strong. I proceeded to create a customized meridian treatment sequence for him. His meridian treatment sequence involved the eyebrow, under the nose, under the lip, and under the arm. I asked him again to think about his dental anxiety and he tested strong on muscle testing. I took him through the 9-Gamut Treatment and repeated the sequence of tapping the eyebrow, under the nose, under the lip, and under the arm. I asked him to think about his dental anxieties again and found that he tested strong. We finished with the Eye Roll. He reported that his SUD level was between one and two.

I muscle tested him for the duration of self-treatment required for the treatment to be permanent and the answer was three times a day for eight weeks. I reviewed the customized meridian treatment sequence with him in reverse to let him know the meaning of the customization. I stated that the core meridian that was affected was the Spleen located under the arm. "Something happened to you which caused you to feel very fearful and this also led you to have realistic anxieties about your future." The second meridian that was affected was the Conception Vessel located under the lip. "The second feeling that came up for you as a result of the fear you initially experienced was shame and some shyness." The third meridian that was affected was the Governing Vessel under the nose. "The feeling that came up for you as a result of the fear and the shame was that you felt embarrassed, as though you had given away your power." The most superficial meridian affected was the Bladder located at the inner portion of the eyebrow. "This feeling of fear and shame and embarrassment went on to make you feel restless, impatient and frustrated with the trauma that you had experienced."

This assessment was eye opening for the participant as he admitted that his extrovert behavior is a way to hide his true self, who is shy, often feels unable to assert his opinion, and somewhat impatient.

Participant Two

Participant Two is a sixty-nine-year-old male. When asked to rate his SUD level around dental treatment he stated the following: "Now that you've been my dentist for a while, I'm much less afraid. So now I'm at a level seven. However, before you became my dentist my level of anxiety was a ten." Because the participant felt more relaxed with me as his dentist, I asked him to think about his dental anxiety prior to becoming my patient, for the duration of this treatment.

When Participant Two was first seen in my office, he avoided eye contact with me, hardly spoke to me, and was sweating extensively while I was performing a non-invasive treatment (in-office teeth whitening) on him. After this treatment, he did not return to my office for a few years. Upon his return, I started treating him for simple procedures such as check-ups, x-rays, and cleanings. With the completion of each appointment he felt more and more at ease as we built trust. At one particular appointment, which involved preparing a tooth for a crown, he repeatedly questioned me on how long it would be before I was done. Similar to a small child sitting in the car wanting to know when he's reached his destination, the participant was very persistent in repeating his question, "Are you done yet?" every few minutes. I finally responded by saying "I'm done when I stop drilling!"

At that point, we both stared at each other in disbelief and started to belly laugh uncontrollably and continued to remember this as an icebreaker during each appointment going forward. Participant Two has a long list of triggers that contribute to his fear and anxiety of dental treatment. He fears not being able to breathe, coughing, choking, claustrophobia, fear of the unknown (not knowing if there will be additional treatment needed, extra cost, extra time), not being completely numb, feeling the pain, the dentist slipping, the fear of the injection, and the needle (insertion discomfort, movement of the needle inside the tissue, pain associated with the injection, hitting a nerve or vein), being surprised, time factor (inconvenient, going on forever, never ending) and bad taste.

After testing him on being centered on all three vectors of energy, I proceeded to check for psychological reversals. The first reversal that was uncovered was Willingness which cleared after tapping on the third eye chakra. The second and last reversal that was uncovered was Permission, which cleared after tapping on the crown chakra. Muscle testing indicated that all the reversals had been successfully cleared.

He reported his SUD level at five. I muscle tested him while asking him to think about his dental fear and anxiety and he tested weak. I proceeded with the creation of the customized meridian treatment sequence. The sequence that emerged involved the eyebrow, outer eye, and under the eye. Tapping on each meridian point while thinking about his dental anxiety and breathing treated all these points. He muscle-tested strong while thinking about the dental anxiety, so we performed the 9-Gamut Treatment and sandwiched that with another series of tapping.

I asked him to think about the problem and he muscle tested strong. His SUD level was between one and two. This indicated that the problem had been resolved and we finished by doing the Eye Roll. After the Eye Roll, he reported his SUD level being at one.

I muscle tested him to find the duration of self-treatment needed to bring about permanent release of the problem and the answer was five times a day for six weeks. I reviewed the customized meridian treatment sequence with him in reverse to let him know the meaning of the customization. I stated that the core meridian that was affected was the Stomach Meridian, whose treatment point is located under the eye. "This means that something happened that produced a lot of fear and anxiety for you. This resulted in you feeling disappointed and bitter and sometimes even a bit nauseous." The second meridian that was affected was the Gall Bladder Meridian whose treatment point is located at the outer eye. "That initial fear and anxiety over time made you furious." The most superficial meridian that was affected was the Bladder, whose treatment point is located at the inner part of the eyebrow. "That initial fear and anxiety which led to you feeling rage and fury finally resulted in you feeling traumatized and very restless, impatient, and frustrated."

Participant Three

Participant Three is a twenty-two-year-old male. This participant reports never having had a cavity and yet reports his SUD level as being seven. During his initial interview, I asked if he remembers ever having a bad experience in a dental office. He responded by saying "no." We continued to discuss what makes him anxious about his dental visits and he reported the following:

When I was a child, my mom told me I had to go see the dentist and I had no say in this. She would wait for me in the waiting room while I was taken back into the treatment room all by myself. As a child I felt all alone while in the chair amongst people I didn't know. I felt awkward having my mouth open and my personal space invaded by people with yellow masks getting very close to me and in my face. I always anticipate pain, and I

*have never liked the sound of the polishing drill, or the taste of
the polishing paste. When they clean my teeth, I hate the sound
of teeth being scraped. It reminds me of the sound of nails on
the chalkboard. I want to be a good patient and not move, but
my mouth gets so dry, and I want to swallow but I can't because
I don't want to mess up what they're doing.*

I noticed that he was very nervous and this was confirmed
when I tested him to see if he was centered. On the up and down
energy flow, he was reversed. We did the Thymus Thump. After
this, he tested as being centered on all three vectors of energy
flow and much more at ease.

I continued on to test for the presence of psychological
reversals. Muscle testing identified a reversal of Possibility
which was cleared by first tapping the crown chakra and then
the third eye chakra. The next psychological reversal that was
uncovered was Safety, which was cleared after tapping the third
eye chakra.

Muscle testing indicated that all reversals had been
successfully cleared. He reported his SUD at six and I intuitively
knew that he still had a reversal present. I repeated all his triggers
in an effort to remind him of all of them and then muscle tested
him again. This time muscle testing showed the presence of a
psychological reversal. The reversal that was uncovered was
Mini, which cleared after tapping under the nose.

He reported his SUD level to be four. Since his muscle
testing showed all reversals were cleared, I muscle tested
him while he thought about the triggers and he tested weak. I
proceeded to create his customized treatment sequence.

Initially the treatment points involved the eyebrow and
the side of the eye only. When I asked him to think about the

problem and muscle tested him, he tested strong. We proceeded to do the 9-Gamut Treatment and sandwiched that with another set of tapping of the treatment points. I asked him to think about the problem and muscle tested him and he tested strong. So, we did the Eye Roll and he reported his SUD level was at three. Muscle testing indicated that all reversals had been successfully cleared. However, I knew something was missed, so I asked him to think about the problem and all the triggers. I muscle tested him on all the triggers that he had already mentioned and he muscle tested strong on all. Finally, I asked him if there was anything else that was bothering him that he hadn't mentioned yet and he responded as follows:

Yes, all of a sudden that overhead light is bothering me. It is too bright and they're shining it on me as though I'm a specimen being examined.

I muscle tested him while he thought about this trigger and he tested weak. As I tested for the treatment points that needed to be treated, a new sequence emerged as follows: eyebrow, side of the eye, collarbone, thumb, and the middle finger. At this point, I confirmed that he was testing strong when muscle tested while thinking about all the triggers. We did the 9-Gamut Treatment and sandwiched that with another sequence of tapping the treatment points. Muscle testing while thinking about the problem was testing strong so we finished with the Eye Roll. He reported his SUD level to be at one.

I muscle tested him to find the duration of self-treatment needed to bring about permanent release of the problem and the answer was once a day for four weeks.

I reviewed the customized meridian treatment sequence with him in reverse to let him know the meaning of the customization. I explained to him that the core meridian that was affected was the Pericardium located on the radial side of the middle finger. This means "something happened that resulted in you feeling very regretful and stubborn, perhaps because of your mom insisting that you be seen by the dentist despite your resistance. The message was that your opinion, voice, and feelings were not of importance." The next meridian that was affected was the Lung Meridian located at the radial side of the thumb. This means "as a result of the stubbornness and regret building up in you due to having to do something you didn't want to do, it became harder and harder for you to tolerate the situation." The third meridian that was affected was the Kidney Meridian located at the collarbone. This means "the stubbornness, regret, and intolerance resulted in fear and anxiety leading up to and during each dental appointment." The fourth meridian that was affected was the Gall Bladder located at the outer eye. This means "all the previous feelings made you feel rage" and the last and most superficial meridian affected was the Bladder located at the inner part of the eyebrow. This means "you finally felt traumatized and the thought of a dental appointment makes you frustrated and restless." This proved that all the triggers needed to be removed before a person is able to feel a significant reduction in the SUD level.

Sometimes some triggers, such as the overhead lamp, may not be present in the person's radar until all the other triggers have been removed. He looked happy, relaxed, and upon leaving my office he mentioned that he felt great.

Participant Four

Participant Four is a forty-two-year-old male. He rated his SUD level as ten. During his initial interview he listed his dental fears as follows:

I'm very afraid of needles. I was diagnosed with multiple sclerosis when I was twenty-one. Treatment of multiple sclerosis has required getting many shots and now I hate needles in general. I have had to have many painful shots in my stomach and in my back. This has been compounded by the awful feelings I've experienced when getting shots during dental visits. When I was a child, they strapped me down in the dental chair to give me shots, which were very painful. As a result, I felt I had no control. I hate how dental needles once inserted in the tissue have to be moved around. The needles hurt and appear huge. Sometimes I would faint just to escape. The smell of alcohol reminds me of hospitals and doctor's offices where shots are given. The thoughts that run through my head are that nothing good ever happens in a doctor's office, it is burdensome and endless, there is no hope, I have no choice or control, I feel a huge amount of disappointment, and unreal pain.

We started with the Thymus Thump to get him relaxed. He tested correctly on energy flow in all three vectors. I proceeded to check for the presence of psychological reversals. As I started to muscle test, he started to get very emotional and tears started to flow down his face. I stopped and asked him if he wanted a break. He said: "I had no idea this was going to make me feel so deeply. The emotions that I thought I had worked through after years of therapy are re-surfacing again and making me feel so upset." I empathized with him and asked if he felt more comfortable stopping or continuing. He said he wanted to continue but wanted to share some important information with me. He shared the following:

I lost my father to colon cancer when I was ten years old. My mother had to accept financial help from my uncle who sexually abused me until my mother remarried and we moved away. I never had the courage to leave because I was just a kid. I also tolerated his bad behavior because I was afraid that without his support my mother and siblings would be homeless. He is dead now and I'm glad he's gone. When I was twenty-one, I was diagnosed with multiple sclerosis. A psychiatrist who was treating me a long time ago told me that multiple sclerosis is one of those diseases that individuals create for themselves and I never understood why anyone would want to create this for themselves!

Normally hearing this would move me to tears but that day all I wanted to do was to help him. I knew that if I lost my ability to be centered, I would not be in a position to help. As I looked at him – despite the sad story I had just heard – I saw a golden light surrounding him. "Gold is considered a spiritual color – it is the sign of saints or godly beings, as depicted on haloes. Used in healing, gold is an excellent overall aid and protection." [24] Feeling guided by a strong sense of protection and purpose in helping him heal, I asked his permission to continue to muscle test him for the presence of psychological reversals and he agreed.

---

24 Soskin, Julie, *How Psychic are You? 76 Techniques to Boost Your Innate Power.* London: Carroll and Brown Limited, 2002.

Throughout the muscle-testing protocol I felt intuitively connected to him and somehow knew what his answers were before the muscle testing confirmed it. I also felt that his fears of needles paralleled the sexual abuse and it was all connected together.

The psychological reversals that were uncovered were Happiness, Mini, Vengeance and Identity. All these reversals cleared after tapping on the crown chakra. This chakra, set at the top of the head, represents pure thought.

The crown chakra connects one with infinite consciousness, the highest energy in the universe. By expanding the crown, one can tap into the deepest sources of spiritual wisdom."[25] His muscle testing showed that there were no more reversals present.

He reported his SUD level at two. I asked him to think about all the triggers and his muscle tested strong. I wasn't convinced so I repeated all the triggers back to him and then muscle tested him again and this time he tested weak.

I proceeded to create a customized meridian treatment sequence. The treatment points that were involved were first the eyebrow, then the side of the eye, and lastly under the eye. He did the 9-Gamut Treatment followed by another round of tapping. He was muscle tested again while thinking about his problem and he tested strong, so we proceeded to do the Eye Roll. He reported his SUD level at zero. But best of all he said: "All I see is bright pink now!"

Soskin described color pink as being a sign of unselfish love and sensitivity. She wrote that pink is the color of a practicing

---

25   Ibid, 29.

healer[26] or may indicate that spiritual healing is currently being implemented.

I muscle tested him for the duration of self-treatment required for the treatment to be permanent and the answer was once a day for eleven months. I reviewed the customized meridian treatment sequence with him in reverse to let him know the meaning of the customization. I stated that the core meridian that was affected was the Stomach whose treatment point is located under the eye. This meant the following: "What happened in your life when you were only a child produced a lot of fear and anxiety for you. The people in your life who were in a position of authority and trust let you down and left you feeling disappointed. This feeling often makes you feel nauseous." The second meridian that was affected was the Gall Bladder whose treatment point is located at the outer eye. This meant the following: "The fear, anxiety and disappointment over time resulted in you feeling rage and fury." The final and most superficial meridian that was affected was the Bladder whose treatment point is at the inner part of the eyebrow. This means: "The experience of sexual abuse and the needles, the pain, the fear, the anxiety, the rage, and bitterness finally made you feel traumatized, restless and frustrated."

He shared that he continuously suffers from stomach problems and incontinence. He also mentioned that he has a fear of unexpected noises occurring around him, which always startles him causing a state of actual panic and fright. He has a hard time falling asleep at night and once asleep, his sleep is interrupted with disturbing nightmares of people attacking and hurting him. In Living Your Soul's Purpose, Mary Hammond

26   Ibid.

stated that trauma in the body and in the energetic field feels constantly agitating.[27] The clusters of symptoms that are called post-traumatic stress involve hypervigilance, startling, and nightmares, all of which were experienced by participant four.

The psychiatrist who had treated him a long time ago had told him that he had created this disease for himself. I explained that every thought or emotion has a physical effect on the body. A long time ago he chose to stop feeling his emotions. That was when these thoughts and emotions connected in manifesting physically in his body. Therefore, he created a parallel situation in his body wherein through multiple sclerosis he became physically numb and unable to move.[28] At the culmination of the session I truly felt that spiritual healing had indeed taken place and I was grateful to have witnessed it.

Participant Five

Participant Five is a thirty-two-year-old female. Initially she rated her SUD at eight. During the initial interview she stated the following as her fears and anxieties around dental treatment:

The noise of the drill bothers me the most. It seems piercingly loud and unexpected. The x-rays hurt me and make me feel like gagging. When I was a child, I was given laughing gas and that was the most horrible experience I ever felt. I get nervous at the anticipation of not knowing how long a procedure will take.

---

27 Hammond and Crowley, *Living Your Soul's Purpose,* 2008.
28 Holz, Gary, and Holz, Robbie, *Journey to the Heart: Secrets of Aboriginal Healing.* Bloomington: iUniverse, Inc., 2011.

Any time I have provided dental treatment to this participant involving the drill, she has requested to wear headphones with very loud music to drown out the noise of the drill. Her experience with the laughing gas is typical when the laughing gas is not titrated properly when administered and too much is given to the individual. The feeling that ensues is best described as falling in a circling motion down a long dark tunnel with no end in sight. This can be very disturbing to a patient.

When I muscle tested her to see if she was centered on all three vectors of energy, she was reversed on the up and down flow. We went through the Heart Massage and the Thymus Thump, after which she tested correctly on all three vectors.

Muscle testing showed that she had a psychological reversal present. The first psychological reversal that was uncovered was Permission, which was cleared after tapping on the crown chakra. I muscle tested her to see if she had another reversal present and she did not. Her SUD level was four.

I proceeded to muscle test her and she tested weak while thinking about her dental anxiety. I started the process of creating a customized meridian treatment sequence. The sequence that emerged was as follows: eyebrow, side of the eye, and under the eye. She did the 9-Gamut Treatment and sandwiched that with another round of tapping. I muscle tested her while she thought about the problem and she tested strong. She reported her SUD level to be one to two. We finished by doing the Eye Roll, after which her SUD level was one.

I muscle tested her for the duration of self-treatment required for the treatment to be permanent and the answer was three times a day for one week. I reviewed the customized meridian treatment sequence with her in reverse to let her know the meaning of the customization. I stated that the core meridian that was affected was the Stomach whose treatment point was under the eye. "The experience you had when you received too much laughing gas was so scary that it left you with anxiety and bitterness and a sense of disappointment. This experience often makes you feel nauseous." The second meridian that was affected was the Gall Bladder whose treatment point is located at the outer eye. "This means you felt rage and were furious that you were made to feel so scared. This was so unexpected that every time you hear the drill, it reminds you of the overwhelming nature of the laughing gas experience."

The last meridian that was affected was the Bladder whose treatment point is located at the inner part of the eyebrow. "This means you felt traumatized and now each time you have a dental appointment you feel restless, impatient, and frustrated at the thought of experiencing that traumatic event again."

Participant Six

Participant Six is a forty-eight-year-old male. When I asked him to rate his SUD when thinking about his dental anxiety, he reported it to be ten. He has always said to me that the only reason he is able to come to a dental appointment and take care of his teeth is because he has me as his dentist, which is why he has been my patient most of his adult life. When he was a child, his cousin was his dentist and he was very rough with him. He reports the following triggers and anxieties in relation to dental treatment:

I feel claustrophobic when lying in the chair. I hate the sound of the drill, my face being touched and people putting their fingers in my mouth. My cousin was rough and he wouldn't let me say anything. He demanded and forced me to behave and be a good patient. I felt like I had no control and no say in the matter. I'm not afraid of needles but the feeling of being numb brings up feelings of loss of control because I lose the sense of knowing where the dentist is working on and I worry that the numbness will never go away. I don't like the feeling of being out of control and that is why I don't want laughing gas, Valium, music, or shades over my eyes. I need to know that at any given moment I have to run.

Even though the subject had read and signed the informed consent, I felt that before starting the session I had to discuss his feelings about this treatment. He responded very candidly and said the following: "It is all very vague to me. I don't believe in it. If it is so great and so effective, why doesn't everyone offer this treatment?" I answered his questions and he said he was willing to give it a try albeit his disbelief that it can work.

After determining that he was centered on all three vectors of energy, we proceeded to muscle test to see if there were any psychological reversals present. Muscle testing identified a reversal of Happiness, which was treated at the third eye chakra. Both psychological reversals of Permission and Never/ Future cleared after tapping the crown chakra. His muscle testing showed that all reversals had been successfully cleared. However, his SUD level was at five. I reviewed his dental anxieties and each trigger especially his cousin's demeanor and how he treated him with no concern about his feelings. This time muscle testing identified a reversal of Mini, which was cleared after tapping under the lip. His SUD was at two and he had no further psychological reversals.

I proceeded to muscle test him and he tested weak while thinking about his dental anxiety. I found that it was more effective if I reviewed all the subject's triggers out loud before muscle testing, instead of leaving it up to him to think about his anxieties. I continued to create his customized meridian treatment sequence. The treatment points involved were the eyebrow and the outer eye. After tapping these points, we did the 9-Gamut Treatment followed by another round of tapping. He muscle tested strong while he thought about his dental anxiety so we finished with the Eye Roll. His SUD level was at zero.

I muscle tested him for the duration of self-treatment required for the treatment to be permanent and the answer was three times a day for seven weeks. I explained the meaning of the customization to him as follows: "The core meridian that was affected was the Gall bladder whose treatment point is located at the outer eye. Your cousin's behavior made you furious and brought about feelings of rage for you. The next meridian that was affected was the Bladder Meridian whose treatment point is located at the inner aspect of the eyebrow. You felt traumatized and frustrated that your power was taken away from you, that your voice and feelings were silenced and not heard."

I asked him how he felt. He said: "It's strange, I haven't forgotten how my cousin treated me, but I just don't care anymore!"

Results

In all six participants, the psychological reversals that were uncovered were a combination of Misery/Happiness, Motivation/Willingness, Permission, Possibility, Safety, Mini, Vengeance, Identity, and Never/Future. The reversals that were not found were Live/Die, Want, Deservingness, and Deprivation.

In all six participants (one-hundred percent) the eyebrow was identified as a treatment point. Four of the participants (sixty-seven percent) had the combination of eyebrow, outer eye, and under eye as their treatment points and one participant had the eyebrow and the outer eye combination as treatment points. Therefore, five of the participants (eighty-three percent) had the eyebrow and the outer eye identified as treatment points.

The frequency of self-treatment ranged from once a day to five times a day. Three of the participants (fifty percent) had to self-treat three times a day. The duration of treatment varied from one week to forty-four weeks (eleven months). Four of the subjects (sixty-seven percent) ranged from four to eight weeks.

Discussion

Amongst all the treatment points for the meridians, the eyebrow was the only one commonly involved in all six subjects. Eyebrow is the treatment point for the Bladder Meridian. Amongst the negative emotions that ride on the Bladder Meridian is trauma. It can be concluded that all six participants were suffering from trauma in relation to their past dental experiences. This does not infer the absence of fear, anxiety, and phobia. On the contrary, three of the subjects (fifty percent) had the under eye treatment point involved in their customized meridian treatment sequence, which is the treatment point for the Stomach Meridian. The negative emotion riding on the Stomach Meridian is fear, anxiety, and phobia.

Feinstein, Eden, and Craig found psychological reversals to be less common in phobias and more common in some other conditions such as addictions. [29] In the three participants who

---

29   Feinstein, Eden, and Craig, *The Promise of Energy*, 2005.

had under eye treatment point involved (Stomach Meridian/ phobia), only one participant had more than two psychological reversals present. Based on the number of participants treated here, it was not possible to draw a firm conclusion in agreement with the above statement. What was strikingly obvious in all six was the superior effect of repeating all their triggers to them out loud instead of leaving it up to them to think about the triggers silently.

As shown by Participant Three, it is paramount that all the triggers are cleared before any significant reduction in SUD is seen. In his case, the overhead lamp was not even mentioned as a trigger during his initial interview. It was not until all the other triggers had been cleared, that the overhead lamp trigger was exposed as an existing trigger for the participant.

As mentioned in Chapter 2, "Trauma has neurological as well as energetic roots. This neurological/energetic symbiosis holds physical pain and illness, disturbed emotion, and irrational limiting thoughts. Trauma, as we understand it in psychology and science today is the interaction of neurology and behavior as a result of being victimized or witnessing a traumatic event."[30]

This was evident in participant four who had experienced sexual abuse. "When a current event reminds the person consciously or unconsciously of the original traumatic event(s) the brain gets stuck, so to speak, in the fight or flight response, and reacts to the reemerging fear with anger or isolation."[31] The fight or flight response is strongly prevalent in patients with dental trauma, as they are either ready to run away, or are

---

30 Hammond and Crowley, *Living Your Soul's Purpose*, 2008, 35.
31 Ibid.

ready to be accusatory, combative, and angry, or even verbally abusive with the dentist or the auxiliary staff.

I had the pleasure of following most of the participants who were my patients over a four-year period and saw individuals who fell asleep during their dental visits instead of white knuckling it through their appointments. They were even able to tolerate lengthy appointments without becoming anxious and forlorn. What was most rewarding for me was an unspoken look in their eyes where they knew that I was always on their side.

I'm confident in stating that customized meridian treatment sequence offers rapid, cost effective, and long-lasting reduction in dental fear and anxiety as compared to other modalities available today. As stated in the experiences of the participants, this modality does not erase the memory of the traumatic event, but instead erases the emotional signal attached to the memory. This treatment is highly valuable not only for the patient, but for the dentist and his/her entire team.

According to Karl Augustus Menninger, "Fears are educated into us, and can if we wish, be educated out." However, this is only true if our patients are aware of their fears. In my experience it's always easier to help a patient who freely admits and is aware of their dental fears and anxieties. It is often most difficult to help those patients who are not aware or who cannot shine a light on those fears and anxieties by admitting their suffering.

As is evident, delivering excellent dentistry is sometimes not possible without educating your patients. Always invite your patients and hold a safe space for them so they can talk to you about their fears.

What keeps your patients awake, the night prior to their dental appointment is what directly affects your success as a dentist and business owner.

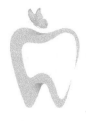

CHAPTER 14:

Four-Minute Protocol Reduces Dental Anxiety by 35 Percent

Dentists know that because of the nature of our practices, we always have to be in a state of preparedness, whether it is for emergencies or a scheduled treatment not proceeding exactly as we planned, or a myriad of other deviations. A patient may arrive at five p.m. on a Friday afternoon requiring emergency treatment and you may be the only office who answered the phone and agreed to see them. What you may not know is that this person is terrified of everything about dental treatment. This fact alone will make the appointment that much more difficult. Creating a customized meridian treatment sequence takes time, which you don't have when faced with treating an anxious and fearful patient experiencing extreme pain.

With this in mind, I sought to create a sequence of meridian tapping that was both effective in alleviating dental fear and anxiety and simple to do. My vision included simplicity so that any member of the dental team would be able to help to calm down an anxious patient without taking time away from the dentist (who might be helping another patient). This helps greatly with not interrupting the flow of a busy dental practice.

As mentioned previously, Gary Craig developed the "original" Basic Recipe for EFT. To illustrate, the example of a client who is afraid of the sound of a dental high-speed drill is used. In this method, the client thinks about a specific memory or event referred to as "Attunement." SUD level is checked and recorded. The client is then taken through the set-up, which involves repeating out loud three times the set-up statement "Even though I have this fear of the loud noise that comes from the dentist's drill, I deeply and completely accept myself," while tapping on the side of the hand or massaging the sore spot. This is followed by tapping the full sequence of points (top of the head, eyebrow, side of eye, under the eye, under the nose, chin, collarbone, under arm, side of ribs, the radial sides of the thumb, index finger, middle finger, and little finger, and finally the Gamut Spot) while stating a reminder phase (such as "loud noise" or "this piercing drilling noise.") The Gamut Spot is tapped while doing the 9-Gamut procedure (close eyes, open eyes, look down to the right corner, look down to the left corner, roll eyes full circle one way, roll eyes full circle opposite way, hum a tune twice, count from one to five, hum a tune twice again. The entire sequence is tapped again while stating the reminder phrase. The client is asked to attune to the problem and the SUD level is recorded. If SUD has not decreased significantly, another set-up phrase is chosen such as "Even though a part of me is still afraid of the drill noise, I love and completely accept myself," while tapping on the side of the hand. This protocol is continued until SUD level is reduced to zero or one.

Although not as lengthy as the customized meridian sequence, the Basic EFT recipe is still quite lengthy for the purpose of providing anxiety relief for a patient requiring urgent dental treatment. In order to determine a shorter self-administered sequence of tapping to alleviate dental fear and anxiety I decided to eliminate all the steps except attuning to the problem and chose only seven acupressure points to tap. Patients were invited to gently tap on the selected seven acupressure points for a total duration of four minutes in the following sequence:

EB = Beginning of Eyebrow
SE = Side of Eye
UE = Under Eye
UN = Under Nose
Ch = Chin
Th = Thumb
BF = Baby Finger

Abbreviations for the acupressure points were derived from Gary Craig.[32] The hypothesis was that dental fear and anxiety can be significantly reduced by using a variant of EFT involving attuning to the problem and tapping the above seven selected acupressure points without verbalizing cognitive affirmations.

The reason I chose the first three acupressure points (EB, SE, and UE) was because the results of a prior study done by this author in 2013, determined that sixty-seven percent of the

---

32 Craig, Gary, *The EFT Manual: Second Edition*. Santa Rosa: Energy Psychology Press, 2008.

individuals in the study suffering from moderate to severe dental fear and anxiety, identified a combination of inner eyebrow (EB), side of eye (SE) and under eye (UE) acupressure points as treatment points for dental anxiety.

Based on the findings of Diamond[33], treatment points can be traced to the affected meridian with disrupted flow and the meridian is then associated with the negative feelings that resulted in the disruption of energy flow. In the above three treatment points the negative feelings that resulted in the disruption of energy flow in the affected meridians were as follows: Restlessness, impatience, frustration, and trauma resulted in disruption of energy flow in the Bladder Meridian for which EB acupressure point is the treatment point. Negative feelings of rage, fury, wrath, frustration, and indecision resulted in disruption of energy flow in the Gall Bladder Meridian whose treatment point is SE. Negative feelings of anxiety, fear, disgust, disappointment, bitterness, greed, deprivation, and nausea resulted in disruption of energy flow in the Stomach Meridian whose treatment point is UE.

The above three treatment points were added to four others in an effort to treat additional residual feelings that might be reported by patients suffering from dental anxiety. Tapping UN resolves feelings of embarrassment, inferiority, and powerlessness caused by disturbances in the flow of energy in the Governing Vessel, tapping the chin resolves feelings of shame caused by disturbances in the Conception Vessel, tapping the thumb resolves feelings of intolerance caused by disturbances in the Lung Meridian and tapping the BF resolves feelings of anger caused by disturbances in the Heart Meridian.

---

33 Diamond, *Life Energy*, 1985.

In order to test the above hypothesis, I did a research study in 2016 to evaluate the efficacy of a self-administered variant of the standard EFT (Emotional Freedom Technique) protocol that the dental practitioner is able to offer patients to reduce their dental anxiety. The results of this study were published in the *Journal of Energy Psychology*.[34] For the details and a copy of this article, please send me a request by going to my website at www.DrBitaSaleh.com.

Eight healthy individuals with dental anxiety, five males, and three females, seventeen and one-half to sixty years old were randomly selected to participate in this study. Four were assigned randomly to the control group (reading a neutral magazine article) and four to the treatment group (tapping the seven assigned treatment points). The study was conducted at my private dental practice in Santa Ana, California as well as over the phone with the individuals present at their residences in the United States. STAI 6-item short form was used to measure the level of self-reported dental anxiety before and after treatment.

Spielberger State-Trait Anxiety Inventory (STAI) is one of the most widely used measures of general anxiety and is available in various languages. This is a self-report questionnaire that is administered by the participant using pen and paper. Specific instructions are provided on the form for each of the questions.

The original STAID (State-Trait Anxiety Inventory for Adults) instrument was developed by Charles Spielberger in 1968 and is a copyrighted instrument. The manual was published in 1983. The original instrument contained forty

---

34 Saleh, Tiscione, and Freedom, *Energy Psychology Journal*, 9 No. 1 (2017) 26-38.

items, subdivided equally into State and Trait anxiety sub-scales. According to Spielberger,[35] the S-anxiety scale evaluates how participants feel at the moment of completing the questionnaire. The T-anxiety scale assesses how people generally feel and establishes a longstanding trait or characteristic. As such, the T-Anxiety is less responsive to change compared to the S-Anxiety, which is why Marteau and Bekker[36] used six of the questions in the state subset of the anxiety scale to create the short form of the questionnaire.

With the permission of the publisher, Mind Garden, I used the six-item short form to assess the dental anxiety of the participants. This questionnaire is quick to administer and does not require costly, or lengthy and complicated scoring or interpretation procedures.

The total duration of this study for each individual was twelve minutes with the specifics as follows: stating name three times and obtaining verbal permission to start (one minute), discussion of dental anxiety triggers specific to the participant (two minutes), interviewer repeating the triggers out loud (two minutes), completion of the questionnaire by the participant (thirty seconds), interviewer repeating the triggers out loud (two minutes), participant reading/tapping (four minutes), completion of the questionnaire by the participant (thirty seconds).

---

35 Spielberger, Charles D., *Manual for the State-Trait Anxiety Inventory for Adults (Forms Y1 and Y2)*. Menlo Park: Mind Garden, 1983.

36 Marteau, Theresa, and Bekker, Hilary, The development of a six-item short-form of the state scale of the Spielberger State-Trait Anxiety Inventory (STAI). *British Journal of Clinical Psychology,* 31(Pt 3), (1992): 301–06.

Upon completion of the study, the anxiety of the control group was reported to have improved by six percent and the treatment group by thirty-five percent. The results show that this self-administered sequence of acupressure tapping by itself (without cognitive affirmation) is an effective, quick, and cost-effective treatment that can be offered to dental patients suffering from dental anxiety. In addition, it can be easily delegated to auxiliary staff prior to start of dental treatment. This improvement also shows that tapping IS the active ingredient in resolving the problem.

A thirty-five percent improvement in dental fear and anxiety is the difference between a dentist not being able to treat a patient vs. the patient being able to sit in the dental chair with a fair amount of ease and comfort long enough for the dentist to perform an emergency treatment.

Whereas the results look most promising, the limitations of the study are as follows: (1) very small sample consisting of eight participants, (2) short duration (single session with each participant, and (3) need to follow through with the next study in which actual dental procedures will be practiced on patients and anxiety studied again to see if it remains mitigated by EFT in the "real-life" situation.

Even with the above limitations, use these methods, and make your own observations as to whether it is helpful in mitigating dental fear and anxiety.

In order to address the patient's overall health (especially in consideration of oral health being related to systemic health) it is prudent to consider mind body approaches such as EFT to treat anxiety. It is by influencing these subtle energetic pathways, through which the life force follows, that EFT is successful in affecting and reducing dental anxiety. In other words, the key to lessening dental anxiety lies in the relationship between energy disruptions in the higher energetic systems caused by negative emotions, and the physical matter.

Both the science of dentistry and advancements in technology have made great strides in advancing patient diagnosis and treatment. However, when the majority of the population avoids seeking dental care due to dental anxiety, the scope of influence for these advancements is limited. Instead of relying heavily on technology to improve patient care, it is valuable to consider both physical and subtle energetic components of a human being.

If our patients are too afraid to sit in our dental chair how can we do the dentistry that we spent years learning to do so well? If eighty percent of the population doesn't care to sit in a beautiful operatory with all the high-end technological advancements costing $100,000 (approximate cost of one treatment room in a dental office) to build, is it worth spending the money needed to build it? It's not that eighty percent of the population will make a conscious decision to not care, and certainly they will see the operatory, but they will not see its beauty and they will not appreciate the high-end equipment because all they are able to see is a torture chamber where they will experience pain. It's just simple logic that in order to do our best dentistry and to be able to fully utilize the amazing technology, we need our patients to be able to sit in our chairs and withstand the entire length of treatment with ease and comfort.

I tell my clients all the time that the best way to cut down on their overhead is to learn how to effectively alleviate their patients' fears and anxieties. The best way to do this is not by spending thousands of dollars on the best music or video system to create a calm environment or on an interior designer to create the same or having beautiful art on the ceiling that the patient can see when laying down in the chair and the list goes on.

Regardless of how much of your hard-earned dollars are spent making the interior of your office calming and spa-like, you will never be able to compete with what is going on in the patient's memory. There is just no competition there unless you learn how to effectively remove the charge carried by those memories.

Most dentists practicing in this day and age have beautiful spa-like offices but not every dentist has the knowledge and the expertise to care for their patients at such deep and powerful levels, which should be a pre-requisite in every patient's care.

I have said this before but it's worth repeating again. The advantage of dental anxiety being handled effectively within the clinical setting is that the level of trust between the dentist and the patient improves exponentially. This, in turn, results in an increased number of patients seeking treatment and improved compliance in addition to patients seeking oral health recommendations from their dentist, instead of incorrectly placing value in the limited coverage offered by insurance companies.

CHAPTER 15:

Operation and Ethics for Dentists Treating Dental Fear and Anxiety with Energy Psychology Methods

In dentistry, we have more than our share of rules and regulations, all meant to protect our patients, employees, and ourselves; but above all, these rules and regulations serve as a compass for us to always, at any given moment, know right from wrong and to have the courage to ask questions when something lacks clarity. These questions allow our profession to evolve with the intention of always doing better for our patients than we did the day before.

As a dentist, your license and training do not authorize you to diagnose and treat mental disorders, as defined by DSM (Diagnostic and Statistical Manual of Mental Disorders).[37]

---

37 American Psychiatric Association, *Diagnostic and Statistical Manual of Mental Disorders, 5th Edition: DSM-5*. Arlington: American Psychiatric Publishing, 2013.

However, patients who suffer from dental fear and anxiety and who can benefit from the methods discussed in this book in relation to their dental treatment, do not necessarily fit into clear categories.

The scope of your practice allows you the foundation to respond appropriately to a patient whose dental fears and anxieties inhibit them from obtaining the proper dental care. Most of the patients that you see for dental treatment (who suffer from dental fear and anxiety) are not willing to see a mental health professional. In fact, some patients may become so offended at such a recommendation that they may leave your practice altogether. It's critical to recommend that this option is available to them, but to also add that you can help alleviate these negative feelings through meridian tapping that focuses only on addressing your patient's ability to undergo dental treatment without experiencing fear and anxiety. This clearly states your intention and boundary for this type of work.

With the help of an attorney who is well versed in energy methods and your state's laws prepare an informed consent form that the patient can read and sign. This form should clearly disclose that you are not a licensed mental health professional and when helping to alleviate their fears and anxieties in relation to dental treatment, you're not acting as their dentist (a profession where you do hold a license). It should be clear that meridian tapping is primarily intended to alleviate fears and anxieties in relation to dental treatment and thus intended to supplement the dentistry that you are licensed to provide. To better illustrate this point, if one of your dental patients who has zero dental fear and anxiety approaches you with the question of whether you can help him with his fear of swimming, it would be best to decline, and instead refer him to a licensed mental health care professional.

It is helpful to know whether your patient is under the care of a licensed mental health care professional or not. If they are, with your patient's permission, it would be best for you and their therapist to work together as an integrated team.

In alignment with the above point and to draw a clear boundary between your dental practice and meridian tapping, conduct the meridian tapping sessions in a consultation room or somewhere in your office where you do not perform dental treatment. Keep this practice completely separate from your dental practice including the payments that these patients make to you for the meridian tapping. As an example, do not use the same credit card machine to accept payment for meridian tapping because it will be deposited into the business account for your dental practice.

Become certified so that you have the confidence to provide this treatment effectively. Also obtain insurance coverage, which is extremely inexpensive in comparison to dental malpractice coverage.

Any records that belong to a client should be placed in a chart separate from their dental chart. The time period in which you keep these records should be ten years from the last time this client had a session with you for the meridian tapping. To be on the safe side, keep the records for ten years plus one day after the client's last dental appointment and meridian tapping appointment, whichever is the most recent.

What you charge is completely up to you. However, charge a fee that allows a high amount of perceived value and proper exchange for your patients. It also prevents you from feeling resentful of giving your time away. Make certain from the beginning that your patient understands that this is purely an out-of-pocket expense that cannot, directly or indirectly, be billed to medical or dental insurance.

Confidentiality rules that apply to your dental practice should apply here as well. Don't have another team member be present while you're treating your patient (including team members taking notes for you). By doing so, you're introducing another person's energy into the room where none is needed.

Make sure that whoever in your office starts the treatment will be the one finishing the treatment. The same rules that apply to you, in regard to being trained correctly and providing proper informed consent, will apply to this team member. Therefore, it's prudent to choose someone who has already proven their loyalty to you and your office. In addition, you need to be present in the office any time this team member is holding a session, for the same reason that you would not allow your dental hygienist working in your office without your direct supervision.

Ultimately, it is your office and if you do not have a satisfactory outcome the responsibility lies heavily on you and no one else. On another more positive note, I can't tell you how excited the auxiliary staff feel about this protocol. You can offer this training to them as a benefit and they will appreciate and love you more than any other benefit will. If your team is excited, not only will they be happier, but their loyalty increases in direct proportion. As they talk about it to your patients, the rate of acceptance for this treatment will be higher. A happy doctor is a doctor with a happy team, happy patients, and a productive office. These individual outcomes are in reality, interdependent factors in the circle of life of a dental practice.

To maintain continuity of flow during a session maintain a quiet area so that you or your patient are not distracted. Unless an emergency arises that needs your immediate attention, tell your entire team to not disturb you during a session.

It is difficult to go back and forth from a dental appointment into these sessions. If you can, schedule the sessions for these patients during a day or half-day that is dedicated to only these sessions.

If you are breaking up a customized meridian tapping session into three appointments allow sixty minutes per session. If you're doing the entire treatment in one session, allow ninety minutes only once you have gained confidence and completed treatment for at least ten practice clients.

In summary, the ethical practices that apply to your dentistry apply equally to your meridian tapping. The health and wellbeing of your patients is always paramount in every decision and treatment recommendation. Being truthful, non-judgmental, and speaking with clarity are all important attributes to hold. The discussion of ethics can go on forever and be a book by itself. Only limited points have been discovered here for the intention of providing the dental practitioner with a few ethical foundations.

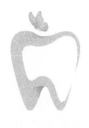

CHAPTER 16:

Obstacles

"This being human is a guest house.
Every morning a new arrival.

A joy, a depression, a meanness,
some momentary awareness comes
as an unexpected visitor.

Welcome and entertain them all!
Even if they're a crowd of sorrows,
who violently sweep your house
empty of its furniture,
still, treat each guest honorably.
He may be clearing you out
for some new delight.

The dark thought, the shame, the malice,
Meet them at the door laughing,

And invite them in.

Be grateful for whoever comes,
Because each has been sent
As a guide from beyond."
– Rumi

The human experience in its entirety includes all emotions, the good as well as the bad. The ones that we wish to evade and so repress always come back again and again with a vengeance, demanding all of our attention. Each emotion exists to bring us a new awareness. Rumi brings to light the messiness of the human experience. The similarity in the methods described in this book and Rumi's poem highlight the importance of being aware of how unpleasant feelings (fear and anxiety) and how through love and acceptance (I totally love and accept myself even though I have this problem.), we release these negative feelings from the prison of our minds.

How many times have you been to a continuing education meeting where you learned an amazing new way of improving patient care and profitability, so much so that upon returning this was the first thing you shared with your team? One month later, you look back and wonder if that amazing new way that you were so excited about was just a dream. You finally realize that the only real tangible evidence you have remaining of that amazing new way is the payment that was deducted from your bank account. So, you ask why. Why did that great way of improving patient care and profitability, never see the light of the day, despite your enthusiasm to the contrary? The only answer that appeases you is to chalk it up as being a great idea that you will implement someday – just not today.

When you've been given the keys to something amazing (improved patient care and profitability), it's up to you to take the keys and open the lock that's on the door in order to reach that amazing something. That amazing something will not be reachable if in the haste of your enthusiasm, you forget to share a copy of the key with your team. Consider for a moment the example of preparing a tooth for a crown, which is not very different to the above situation. Even though you're the only one in your office licensed to perform the treatment, all members of your team know the steps required for crown preparation and cementation. When a patient comes to the front to reserve their appointment, your front office knows exactly what procedure to book them for and the required length of the procedure. When your patient shows up for the procedure your front office knows how much to collect and the assistant knows how to set up for the procedure.

The magic for the successful implementation of this method occurs when you train your entire team and they get to practice on one another. When they agree to undergo this treatment as a practice client, they will experience firsthand how powerful and profound the effects are. They will share their enthusiasm by talking to their family and friends and to your patients. This is how the process sees the light of the day.

This will allow you to have a human connection that goes beyond the regular dental patient appointment. This is when you realize the gold mine that has been hiding in your computer, a whole new set of patients. These are patients you don't have to advertise to gain, because they were already your patients but were avoiding treatment – who are now accepting your recommended treatment.

Unfortunately, with every new and exciting way comes resistance. This is how our brains work. Even with the best of intentions, in order to keep everything the same, your brain will cleverly devise ways to throw you off. The brain naturally believes that change opens the door to the unknown and the unknown is uncomfortable; so, change is considered scary. To demonstrate this, think back on how many times you have recommended treatment that you know will improve a patient's health. Instead of making the appointment, patients avoid making the appointment by telling you that they have to wait on it until they discuss it with their partner or their significant other or their family. They use excuses such as these as a way to postpone what they know deep down they have to do. How many times have you heard your patients talk about changing how they care for their teeth and they don't? How many times have patients scheduled for treatment and end up canceling last minute or worse not showing up at all? Most people will spend their entire lives talking about change and never actually change. They complain because they want whiter teeth but when you propose an in-office whitening treatment they remind you that they said: "someday" and that day is not today. What is really going on is they lack the courage to move forward and do something about what makes them unhappy.

If you take an honest look at the status quo of your practice, I would guess that there is plenty of treatment that you have recommended that doesn't get scheduled. If you add up unscheduled treatment, it would be worth millions. But every month you witness your production to not even closely match the worth of the pending treatment in your patient files. You have late cancellations, and at times, no-shows, which ruin the mood of everyone on your team. You have patients who don't want to pay their copays or who might say that your fees are too high. Then there are others who won't even do their cleanings unless it's covered by their insurance or those who insist on Saturday appointments (because their work doesn't allow time off for dental appointments) only to no-show and not even have the courtesy to call to let you know that they won't be keeping their appointment. Then there are those who don't pay your bill and when you send them to collection, they retaliate by writing you a bad review. Some will leave your practice the minute their insurance changes and they realize you're not a preferred provider on their insurance plan. Some will leave your practice if they move and realize they have to drive an extra fifteen minutes to your office. Unless you practice in a rural area where you're the only dentist within a fifty-mile radius, you will experience all or some of the above. It's because of these reasons and others that you will spend a lot of money advertising in order to attract new patients only to repeat the cycle again and again. Somewhere in the repeating of this cycle you'll realize that your patient retention numbers remain low, so you'll spend money to improve things that won't even matter to your patients. You may decide to hire a reputation management company to help you increase positive reviews to drown out the negative ones and there will always be more reasons to add to your overhead when the real reason is hiding right under your nose. In the case of specialists, you might feel unhappy because you're not getting enough referrals from general dentists. Whatever is keeping you awake at night is what you need to get help for. Don't let the "someday" syndrome" come between you and the support that you need in order to catapult you to the practice of your dreams where stress is no longer running the show.

Lastly, know that the same obstacles that your patients experience when scheduling for treatment are the same ones that you will experience when you are considering doing a substantial training. I have seen unnatural forces come into play. One client experienced flooding of his entire basement so the money he had saved for training had to be spent fixing his basement and the list goes on. These are all the result of resistance that your mind creates to divert you off the path of change. Once you decide firmly and commit to the training all the resistance takes a back seat waiting to come forth again for the next change. It's in the spaces in between resistances that transformation happens.

I hope that you won't look at this book as the next best idea that you will get to "someday," while you unhappily tolerate the stress of running a practice (where most of the patients are too fearful to get healthy) and postpone living your career to its full potential.

The minute that you decide to be courageous enough to do things differently will be the moment that your patients will do the same.

CONCLUSION

In her book, *A Return to Love: Reflections on the Principles of a Course in Miracles*, Marianne Williamson wrote about the fear of living life to its full potential:

> *"Our deepest fear is not that we are inadequate.*
> *Our deepest fear is that we are powerful beyond measure.*
> *It is our light, not our darkness, that*
> *most frightens us."*[38]

At the beginning of this book, I raised the question of why as dentists we have been silent for so long. The reason is that the most critical factor in treating patients successfully lies outside the scope of our practices. So even though we know that our patients struggle with fear and anxiety, we remain quiet because the choices available to us are limited: either offer sedation or hope for the best.

We are frustrated because our patients don't listen to us, they don't follow our recommendations, and we can't do our best work when faced with dental fear and anxiety. In our ongoing effort to be better, we attend continuing education classes to

---

38 Williamson, Marianne, *A Return to Love: Reflections on the Principles of "A Course in Miracles."* San Francisco: HarperOne, 1996.

learn how to improve patient care. However, our choices are limited to either advancements in technology, better products, or improved techniques. Mostly this newly acquired interest takes a back seat as we struggle with patients arguing with us over insurance limitations of just a cleaning. We again wonder how it is possible to practice the way we were taught when our patients only want what is covered by insurance, which in this day and age is two cleanings, two exams, a few x-rays, and a couple of fillings per year.

These limitations gradually eat away at the love we once had for dentistry as we realize that what patients want in real life pales in comparison to what we were taught in dental school and in continuing education classes. We realize that no one talked to us about the problem of fear and anxiety in dentistry. We didn't even talk about it amongst ourselves because other than sedation there was nothing else that we could offer to our patients. As the silence increases, the gap widens between our patients and us, and so does the dissatisfaction with a profession that we once loved, as well as the rate of burnout, early retirement, disability, and in some unfortunate cases, the rate of suicide.

As we go home every night, we wonder how things would turn out if there was no insurance. At dental meetings and social get-togethers, we all profess that insurance plans are the cause of most of our stress. We ask the question: "If there was no insurance, would my patients listen to me more?" But we all know deep down that even then, our patients would behave the same. Those who had insurance would have one less ammunition (as if we were the enemy) to throw at us, but they would continue to be the same humans who are scared and not really showing up to our offices as their true selves. It is their fearful part that often makes the decision to remodel their kitchen or go on a vacation instead of saving their teeth.

The feeling of being inadequately trained as dental professionals in relation to treating our patients' fears and anxieties, and viewing them as whole human beings, is shared amongst most dentists. We all want more meaningful and respectful connections with our patients and vice versa. This book provides that missing piece. By alleviating your patients' dental fears and anxieties you will be able to change the way you practice now to the way you loved to practice when you got out of school before the grind made you bitter. You will no longer give up on some patients and they won't give up on you and their dental health.

I have candidly shared parts of my story and the reasons why I have been searching to find a way to alleviate the fears and anxieties experienced by so many patients. I have been there where you are in the trenches and I am confident that you can master these methods successfully. For me it was a gift to discover that I could finally alleviate my patients' fears and anxieties quickly and conservatively. As someone who felt all my patients' fearful feelings as though the terror was my own, on the road to saving them, I saved myself as well. For the dentist, the result is to practice the excellent dentistry that we were taught, be respected and heard by our patients, see the loyal patients that we've built relationships with return year after year, and to see our efforts lead to abundant profitability. For the patient, the result is to receive dental care with ease and comfort and to reap the rewards of dental health.

Every day of my career, I started my day with one question: "How may I serve today?" Every evening, I asked the same question with a slight modification: "How well did I serve today?" The effectiveness of my ability to serve my patients was directly related to not only my knowledge and expertise, but also to how I felt, physically and emotionally. I hope that you use the techniques described in this book both to serve your patients, and the one person who needs it the most, that being yourself.

Fear is a natural response that is meant to protect us from harm. However, when that fear has been transformed into a negative belief it becomes an inner voice and barrier that continually whispers that change is unacceptable but being stuck is better – it's more familiar! This prevents us from stepping into who we really and honestly deep down want to be. As this voice pushes us back each time we want to grow and reach a goal, we watch our dreams remain just that, a dream. Our patients can't live their lives fully if they're constantly afraid of how their smile looks or how confident they feel in their speech. Their dental health affects their relationships as well as their success at work and home. As parents, as friends, as employers and employees, as entrepreneurs, every second of every day, they are using their teeth to function and be someone they can be proud of. Helping them overcome their dental fears and anxieties, so that they can feel confident in making every day decisions and taking critical actions, allows them to live a life that is full of courage and abundance instead of fear and scarcity.

Remember this method of treatment allows a bond to be created between you and your patient at a level that is otherwise impossible to achieve. They will feel that you see them for who they truly are outside of their fears and anxieties. They will know that no one cares for them as much as you do and will remain loyal to you for all their years. They will also accept your treatment recommendations without their insurance coverage acting as the gatekeeper of treatment allowance.

They will know that you want nothing but the best for them and you will be the only one they will listen to. Without you even needing to ask, they will refer their loved ones to you. They will embody all the attributes of your ideal patient. The choice to be their ideal dentist or not lies in your willingness to take the time to learn these methods and become certified so that you can bring about this life altering change for your patients.

Following the instructions set forth in this book will allow you to learn and implement these methods in your office. For those who prefer to attain complete proficiency, I offer a personalized coaching program where you can work with me to learn and implement these methods easily, quickly, and more successfully. To do so, please go to my website, www.DrBita-Saleh.com and submit a request for *The Fearless Way Coaching Program*. Your courage and dedication to your patients, is the reason why no child or adult will ever be traumatized or re-traumatized in a dental chair again.

My wish for you is to know how to identify the red flags of dental fear and anxiety. Such knowing allows you to resolve the fears, anxieties and limiting beliefs of your patients, resulting in a stress-free, profitable, and fulfilling practice that is in balance with your personal life. I look forward to working with you so that I can witness you achieving these results and more in real-life.

ACKNOWLEDGEMENTS

One week after handing in my writing assignment, I was rushing to make it on time to my English literature class, which happened to be one of my favorite classes in college. As I was running up the staircase, my college English professor saw me and called out my name loudly to make sure his voice carried over the chattering noises of all the other students. Once he had my full attention he walked over and said: "I read your assignment. Your writing is really good. If you ever decide to write a book you should do it."

I never expected my college professor to walk over to me to tell me my writing was good and that I should write a book someday. After I got over the surprise, I felt incredibly proud, not only because of his encouraging words, but also because he felt it was important enough to seek me out to deliver those words to me in person. I hope he will read this and will know the immensity of the positive impact that his words had in my life.

My love for English literature and writing always competed with my love for science and dentistry. I am forever grateful to my father who encouraged me regardless of what I chose to pursue as a profession.

I want to thank each patient who shared his/her fears and anxieties and enthusiastically participated in the research that made this book possible. You know who you are. I am eternally grateful to you for trusting me.

To my fellow colleagues in dentistry and fellow coaches at CTI, thank you for supporting my quest and believing that the world was ready to receive and in need of this body of work.

To the Morgan James Publishing team: Special thanks to David Hancock, CEO & Founder for believing in me and my message. To my Author Relations Manager, Gayle West, thanks for making the process seamless and easy. Many more thanks to everyone else, but especially Jim Howard, Chris Howard, Bethany Marshall, and Nickcole Watkins.

Last, but not least, I owe my dog, Pumpkin, a world of gratitude, for sitting by my side while I wrote the pages of this book, with infinite patience and love.

THANK YOU

Thank you for reading!

The fact that you have reached this point tells me something very important about you: You are committed to your profession and you care deeply about the wellbeing of your existing and future patients - so much that you're ready to step into making a significant difference in their lives.

I can't wait for you to see your profitability increase exponentially as you offer *The Fearless Way Program* as a service to your patients. The best part is seeing the look in your patient's eyes, when for the first time in their lives, they no longer feel paralyzed with fear at the thought of facing dental treatment.

To show my appreciation to you for reading this book and to support you in beginning the implementation of *The Fearless Way Program* in your practice, please visit my website at www. DrBitaSaleh.com to download the following "Anxiety-Free" freebies.

1. Check list of steps A-Z to keep you organized while implementing *The Fearless Way Program* in your practice.

2. Sample letters to send to patients and referral sources to introduce *The Fearless Way Program* as a service provided in your practice.

3. List of my favorite resources.
4. A copy of my published article: *The Effect of Emotional Freedom Techniques on Patients with Dental Anxiety: A Pilot Study.*
5. To discover if your practice is missing out on scheduling potential fearless patients every day, request your Free Secret Call at www.DrBitaSaleh.com.

ABOUT THE AUTHOR

Bita Saleh, DDS, is a general dentist, author, speaker, coach, and consultant. She is sought after by her clients for personal, leadership, business, and executive coaching.

Dr. Saleh received her Doctor of Dental Surgery degree in 1989 from the University of Southern California School of Dentistry. She then completed a one-year general dentistry residency at Los Angeles County – USC Medical Center.

She has been practicing general dentistry in Orange County for twenty-seven years and was the owner and CEO of her privately-owned dental practice from 1991 to 2017. Her long-standing interest in complementary and alternative medicine led her to complete a certificate in Integrative and Holistic Health (with a concentration in Energy Medicine).

Throughout her career, Dr. Saleh has had an interest in the problem of dental anxiety, which negatively impacts both patients and dentists. She has had her research published, which detailed an innovative four-minute protocol of meridian tapping for alleviating anxiety in dental patients. She is passionate about teaching dentists how to alleviate dental anxiety so that they can enjoy doing the excellent dentistry that they were taught and improve the profitability of their practice(s).

Dr. Saleh has been invited to many speaking engagements, including UCLA School of Dentistry and the research symposium of the Association for Comprehensive Energy Psychology.

She currently lives in Southern California where she devotes her time to teaching, writing, and coaching. For more information about Dr. Saleh, contact her via the following: www.DrBitaSaleh.com and Facebook (Dr Bita Saleh).

Printed in the USA
CPSIA information can be obtained
at www.ICGtesting.com
JSHW022342140824
68134JS00019B/1632